The Force Behind the Stars

The
Force Behind the
STARS

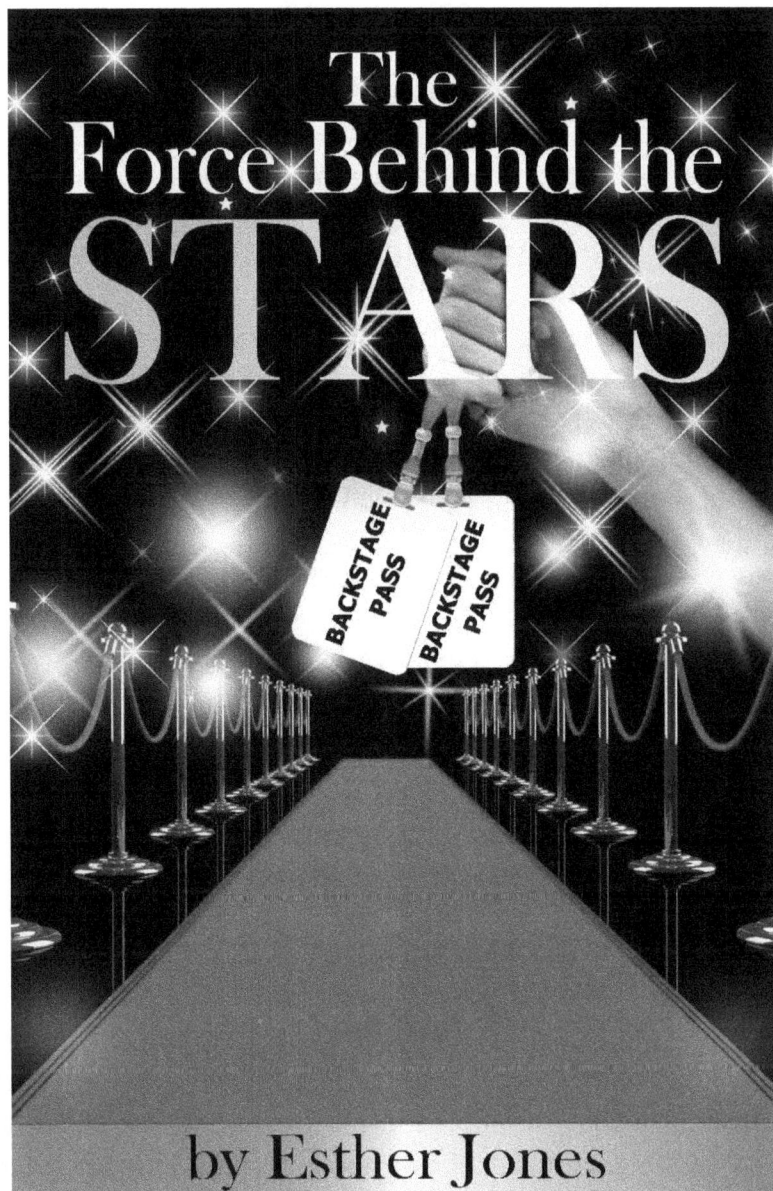

The
Force Behind the
STARS

BACKSTAGE PASS
BACKSTAGE PASS

by Esther Jones

Esther Jones

The Force Behind the Stars

Copyright © 2015
Esther Jones

Printed in the United States of America

Library of Congress – Catalogued in Publication Data

ISBN 978-0692497807

Unless otherwise indicated all scriptural quotations are
taken from the King James Version of the Bible.

Titles of chapters created by Graceson Todd and
Esther Jones

Book design concept by Esther Jones

Published by:
Jabez Books Writers' Agency
(A Division of Clark's Consultant Group)
www.clarksconsultantgroup.com

Jabez Books

• • •

Dedication

This book is dedicated to every celebrity artists suffering in silence. I feel your pain. I see your hurts. I see the betrayal, pressure of press, invasion of fans, sleepless nights, fear of going broke, fear of dying, torment in your mind, identity crisis, suicidal thoughts, and weary from all the pressure of keeping up with this image that the force has trapped you in. I love you and I am here for you. There is a way out. You can come out.

I also dedicate this book to this generation who look up to these celebrities for their identity. Your freedom is here too. All false identities are coming down, so let the real them come forth.

Acknowledgements

To my best friend, the third person of the Trinity, the Holy Spirit. Thank you, precious Holy Spirit for encouraging and commissioning me to write what I have experienced in this book. You are truly the author and publicist of my life.

To my King and Lord Jesus, thank you for the blood that protected me from bullets, being murdered, and dying. You been my ride or die....Let's do this, I got your back, Lord!

To my mommy, Alice Jones, who called me Esther from birth. You always said, "You can do it, you're, Queen Esther!!" Thank you for doing the honors....lol. Your faith sparks mine. Raising 11 children, in the ways of the Lord is what grounded me. Instilling fasting and Bible studying habits are what kept me. Thank you, Mommy.

To my 15 brothers and Sisters and Dad, I love you.

To my big brother, James Jones: Thank you for your overprotective heart. You been my bodyguard since birth. Let's travel the world.

To my friend, Evelyn Sheppard: Thank you for getting on the greyhound with me in the snow that day. Man....Your understanding is amazing. Triple E.

To my Jonathans in my life: Thank you Tiffany Love, Jasmine Curry, and Stephanie Christine for praying me through out and through hell. Your friendship is cherished.

To my Mama/Mentor/Mordechai/Naomi: Brenda Todd: thank you for your long suffering with me.

Thank you for your chastising and pushing me to walk in excellence. I have learned how to be a phenomenal women, wife, and mother from you. Your life of perseverance has taught me how quitting is not an option and your favorite quote to me is "Stop the madness Starla...Let's believe God"

To Jabez Publishing and Dr. Clark: Thank you for what you do for the Kingdom of Light. Hearing your revelation of the marketplace made me realize why I operate how I do. Thank you for the help on this mandate, my book.

To Pastor Natacha Byrams: Thank you for FULLY accepting me. Your love walk is Agape love certified. I have never seen someone who is rooted and grounded in Agape love, speaks the truth in love, and doesn't compromise the Word of God. You taught me about mammon and how to not be ruled by it. Thank you for not using me, not just wanting my money, you wanted my freedom!! Thank you! Thanks for fighting for me, Pastor. We can't be bought! #KingdomKeys

So many in my life has a special place, you know who you are. Loyalty thanks to Natosha Burts, Aeris Gardner, Trinette Lester and Tiara Huddleston.

To Stephanie Christine (chyna whyte) Jasmine and Cory Curry, and Jesus....Let's get these souls!!

Table of Contents

#TheForceBehindTheStars

CHAPTER 1

STARRING AT THE GLASS

Almost everyone had a "blunt" of marijuana and was smoking it, then passing it throughout the crowd as the "West Coast Rapper" performed. A smoky cloud of neon and florescent lights were glazing throughout the room. After the smoke cleared at the "Puff Puff Pass Tour" downtown at the Convention Center in Tulsa, Ok, my friend's beautiful face caught the attention of one of the members of the entourage of the famous "West Coast Rapper."

The guy was dressed in lime green. He carried a "pimp" cane to compliment his outfit. The look he gave her was one I would become all too familiar with. He pointed his cane at her, then at the rest of us, giving us a silent approval to come backstage.

A huge bodyguard moved at the command and node as he escorted us backstage where the many West Coast legends were having what we called a smoke session. I remember it being very cloudy with the smell of fresh Cali (marijuana) in the air. I was young and naïve, but the excitement of being with celebrities were surreal. I didn't smoke back then; I was nervous, and I didn't know what to expect. However, the "weed" was so strong that I began to get dizzy. But it was obvious that the other females that were in the room were used to this routine. And the stares they gave me was one of domineering. I definitely felt out of place backstage. But when the West Coast Rappers started singing a freestyle in the room, I felt more relaxed.

I remember the songs like it was yesterday. And the one that I call, "Mr. Doggy Dog" was giving instructions to his groupies, the do's and don'ts while with him. They all chimed in on the chorus of, "That you don't do." I was more nervous now than ever. I didn't know we had stipulations to being back stage. The rappers Bad A#$#, Corrupt, the two "East Siders" continued to add verses about the rules of engagement with them. I was intrigued by the power and authority Mr. Doggy Dog walked in.

The atmosphere was like he ruled the world and anything he asked for, he could have. There was homage giving to him like I had never encountered before. Also, I met Snoop's Uncle, Uncle Jun Bug, that night and I will never forget the carefree spirit he had.

His love was genuine and sweet. He invited us back to the tour bus to go with them. I was amazed by the non-verbal command they walked in. It was almost like the people were hypnotized that followed his commands.

Snoop Dog lead us out to the tour busses, where the people just lined up and did what he wanted. I could tell the people on the tour knew the after party operations because it shifted with no talking. You see there was definitely a non-verbal communication and authority that the entourage walked in that those who had been around them for a long time knew what it meant.

I saw three girls split to one bus with a guy, then my friend went with one on the bus. Mr. Dog waved as the crowd above the underground garage yelled His name. I remember one of the guys in the group asking my friend to open her mouth, so he could see how deep her throat was. I remember feeling disrespected as if the women were only seen as sex objects. However, the feeling of admiration for the power they walked in made me put up with the disrespect.

The guys were doing their choosing for the night as they picked the other chicks from backstage to go back to the hotel with them. I remember one looking at me and saying, "Not her, she's ugly," with an insulting laugh. I didn't say anything, but just went the other way. I had mud jeans on, and they wore Loui Vuitton. I could feel the judgment based on my brand of clothes, which made me feel like I was nobody. I felt invisible and unwanted; the pain of rejection filled my heart as I looked at everyone else getting on the tour bus. Regardless, this life sure looked wonderful from what I saw in just one night. That life must be a dream come true. Truly it was, and these rappers were gods.

The next morning I was daydreaming so much in school, I couldn't do my work. At the time, I was a senior at Edison High School. I was looking at the autograph Snoop gave me, I noticed he had spelled my name wrong, but it really didn't matter to me at the time. I was just happy about being with celebrities; it definitely made me feel important. But the poisonous words that the entourage spoke over me continued to ring in my head for weeks. He looked at me like I disgusted him.

I was only 18 at the time when the tour came through Tulsa. However, I determined in my heart right then I was going to be somebody important in life. I set out to prove I wasn't ugly and that I truly did have something to offer the world. I would show them I was more than my outfit.

I started to think a lot of critical thoughts about myself, and I had regrets. I thought, *"Why didn't I tell him, I didn't even pay to see him, and that we only came for Snoop."* It was so much I could have said, but didn't, but now I wanted revenge. The next time he would see me, he would be paying me to sit on his face was my thoughts.

It was the fourth of July in Dallas, TX and I took a road trip with Auntie Q, my friends: Lisa, Ramonda, and Mo. By then, I had graduated from High School We planned on going to Six Flags Park, and also to the

Evolution Tour featuring Usher, Nas and Faith Evans, which was in town at the same time.

Auntie Q knew one of the guys that was working on the tour and she arranged for us to meet him backstage to get our VIP passes. We pulled up where all the tour busses were parked. Auntie Q called her connection and he opened the gate to escort us in. He gave us the protocol of being backstage. Our passes included a meet and greet with Nas, front row seats, and free T-Shirts! Mo and I were super excited because he was "fine," and we loved "gangster" rap.

The room we were waiting in was filled with excitement and anticipation. The single "One Mic" was in heavy rotation at the time. I remember wondering how Nas would look in person, and hopefully, he could

sign our free T-shirts.

Then Usher's bodyguard entered the room with

disappointing news that Usher had to do the meet and

greet because Nas was about to perform. I let out a sigh

of disappointment. Mo and I started pouting and

talking "noise" about Usher. We wanted a fine thug not

a R & B singer, so we thought, "Ahhhhhh!" High

screams quieted our complaints as we saw the slim, six-

pack, baby face looking, fine man in front of us with a

crisp white t-shirt and blue jeans on with diamond

blinging earrings in. It was Usher!

Usher does not look the same in person as on

TV. He is much finer and more of a beautiful pretty boy

in person. His cologne made me weak in my knees as I

squeezed Mo hand. His smile was mesmerizing and I remember something in his belly was pulling me toward him.

There were other girls in the room who wanted to take pictures and we were in line to be next. However, I went first. The camera wouldn't snap initially, and his hands holding my side made me weak. I tried not to look at him, so I wouldn't lose my composure. After about 20 seconds of them fixing the camera, I looked at him and gave him a bear hug, snap...they took the picture. I landed all my weight on him and we almost fell over, but he caught us. The bodyguards looked at me in disappointment, then at the one who connected us. The rule goes that whoever brought you in was responsible for your actions. But I really didn't care if I embarrassed them or not, Usher was bigger than life. The security team kindly escorted us out of the room while shaking their heads.

At the concert, we were front and center watching Usher sing while stripping off his shirt. I was mesmerized by his dancing and singing. The women were watching him as wild fantasies were going on in their imaginations. And there it was again, the excitement that I felt in my belly earlier at the meet and greet, from being in the atmosphere of the concert and being seated on the front row. Usher gave the best performance ever. I felt like he was just singing only to me. "You got it bad" song had everyone reminiscing on their old days of being "sprung" on someone.

Usher dancing was seductive and very sexual. The person I just met backstage was gone!!! Who was this? I would soon find out how different the celebrity stars were without the bright lights shining on them on stage. There is definitely something that rises up in them. Because what human can pull people to them?

This pull can make you want to be them and follow them. And whatever is manifested on stage causes thousands of women to offer money and sex to this image. It was something to this music business, and I was extremely curious to find out exactly what it was. My craving to get that kind of power at my disposal is what I left yearning for after the concert was over. I thought to myself, "The world would be mine."

My third experience with the music industry before I decided to get into it was at a Chingy concert in Tulsa, Ok. A lot went on in 2003 concerning my destiny. In my heart there was always a passion for people. I knew about Jesus, and I always had a question in my mind when I met someone, to ask, if they knew Him. But after meeting Snoop and Usher, seeing the authority they walked in, and after encountering the atmospheres at the concerts, thinking about Jesus was the last thing on my mind. I just wanted what they had.

People worshipped them. People clapped for them. People screamed for them. The sound of hand claps for me seemed more intriguing than just telling people about Jesus. I had to find a way in this entertainment business.

The Force Behind the Stars

I was at my friends' Me-Me mom's house in her living room watching music videos one day on her big screen. I saw these rappers with baggy clothes and doing a crazy, silly, fun dance. I heard this fine, light skinned man beneath the St. Louis arch saying, "I'm going down down baby yo street in a Range Rover." I was mesmerized by his charisma. I watched the video every time it came on TV imaging myself through the lyrics in the sound. I had already been to St. Louis in the spirit because the music took me there every time I heard "Nelly's" voice. He was an amazing rapper to me, and I thought, "I would love to marry him."

I bought every magazine he was in, and would paste the poster on my bedroom walls. In my room all you could see was Nelly on every wall. My mom was a minister of the Gospel, and she didn't listen to music that wasn't talking about Jesus. So I couldn't play his music in her house, but in my car was an atmosphere that Nelly created with his lyrics. I was definitely a Nelly fan.

Tulsa is the Bible-belt, so concerts didn't really come through where I lived. In 2003, Chingy's single, "Right Thurr" was hot at the time, and he was doing a show in October in Tulsa. I knew Chingy was from St. Louis because St. Louis people have a certain look and sound. My friend Eve got tickets to the event and we attended it that night. The concert was "cool." It was at a "ghetto" club and people were smoking weed everywhere. The crowd knew every song, but I was just looking as they sung along. I was a party girl, but that night I was just not feeling it.

The concert was over and we headed over to the DoubleTree Hotel. We went upstairs to the 14th floor as we were surrounded with half dressed women giggling and looking for the stars. I remember feeling that excitement again, but I never understood why they wanted to have sex with them after the concerts. Lisa and I sat down in the hallway just "chilling." I was tired and really ready to go home. When a white man came from the back stairway, Lisa gave me the eye signal. He was really cute and nice. He asked us what we were doing in the hallway. I said we were locked out of our room. You see, I was raised with hustlers and pimps for family members who taught me how to "run" games and hustle. I hated it, but it got me whatever I wanted to get. Also, I had a "cold mouthpiece." The influence of my word could convince people to do anything I said. He gave the motion to come with him, we obeyed.

DJ Sno was the guy's name we met in the hallway of the DoubleTree Hotel in Tulsa, OK. It was the "beginning" of my story in the music industry. DJ Sno gave us the rundown of how the industry went. He basically showed us how the inside really operated. He spoke openly of the demands, craziness of fans, and pressure. He not only was down to earth, but a real genuine dude. We felt safe with DJ Sno. He took very good care of us. He even invited us to St. Louis sometime.

Chingy's bodyguard knocked on the door, so I left with him so they could have some privacy. We talked a little in a different hotel room and he started to rub on my thighs. I was not attracted to him, so I frankly told him, "NO I am not a whore, but there are some other pretty women in the lobby who would love to be in the room with Chingy or his entourage." He laughed, then I left.

I was surprised at my words, did I just say I would get a chick for him? Because I wanted to be in the music industry this seemed like a good way to gain favor with them. On my way back on the elevator, Mr. Right Thurr passed with three half-naked girls talking about the different things they were about to do in the room. I saw a look in the girls' eyes that said, "I want to

Esther Jones

feel wanted, I want to feel important, envy me." I actually felt grossed out and sorry for the women who would be forgotten before the rap star plane took off back to St. Louis.

When I got to the floor where DJ Sno was that feeling of rejection came over me again. The feeling of not being included in the after party was getting all too familiar in this music business. I felt the force tugging on me through that crave of acceptance again. It said do whatever you had to do to get the power of influence I had seen.

Their flight was leaving early that morning so the airport van had to leave at 4:00 a.m. from the hotel. I helped DJ Sno with all his bags so he wouldn't get left. I remember seeing Chingy and his two brothers OG and

• • •
36

Rich get in the van as well. The bodyguard said hello, then I gave DJ Sno a good-bye hug, but the rest just stared at me. I was thinking you all looked like normal people who just woke up. What was so different on stage than in person? It was just like with Usher and Snoop, it had to be a force bigger than them that made the concert so exciting – an amazing supernatural high. DJ Sno said thank you as they went out of the gate of Tulsa. A light bulb went off in my brain, the St. Louis gate just opened!!

I wanted in this music thing!!

I didn't just want to stare at the glass anymore.

I definitely was ready to get in...take a sip

...so I thought.

Chapter 2

TAKING A SIP

It was 4:32 a.m., Thanksgiving morning. The snow was coming down heavy on the 44 East Turnpike to the gateway city. We decided to take a last minute trip to the "Lou." This was crazy because we had never been. We didn't know anybody, but DJ Sno. He called for us, so we were for it. It was Lisa, Eve and

I in my sister's car, a grey Alero. I had a Hyundai, but I didn't feel safe in taking it. The girls were asleep and I was in the driver's seat going 100 miles on a pavement covered with snow.

I am surprised we made it in one piece. My eyelids were really heavy with sleep, so I was "pushing" the car even harder. Eve woke up in Rolla, MO and yelled STOP ESTHER! I was always a dare devil, but from the tone in her voice, I knew I was going too far. The hills in Rolla where curvy and the rocks were known to fall. The roads were slick with ice spots so really I had no business speeding over 100mph. But I kept pushing, then I heard a click in the engine. I knew enough about cars that it meant; it was dying. When I saw the St. Louis sign, I felt happy even though the car sounded like it had it, and we did make it to the hotel by sunrise.

When we got settled, we called DJ Sno to see where he was. I was on "cloud nine" in St. Louis. We pulled in at the LaQuinta Inn right by the airport off Highway 70. From that day forward, our favorite spot became the LaQuinta Inn because we got to know the staff and from time to time, we would get free rooms. Also, the drivers at the hotel had a crush on Eve and I, so they took us all around St. Louis. We decided to pick up DJ Sno in the LaQuinta Inn van that day.

When we got back to the room from the airport, Eve and I decided to go see about my sister's car. The car was going 20 miles an hour with a life ending click the whole way. How would we get around St. Louis that weekend? Then we saw a car shop, so we pulled off highway 70 to have them look at it. We called our driver from La Quinta Inn to pick us up from the shop and he did. This whole situation did not look good, though.

When we got back to the room, we found that Lisa was gone. I panicked, then shifted into my gangster mindset. I looked at Eve and thought about calling the police. We didn't know this man or nothing about St. Louis. As we thought about it, we got more and more upset, so I told Eve, let's jump on the bed.

We were in St. Louis for Thanksgiving. We had also heard from the radio 95.5 that Nelly was having a party Friday night. We had to get our plan together. I had to make things happen, then I thought of a plan. We made a song while jumping on the beds --

"Hotel Motel Holiday Inn, if that nigga started acting up

we gon' beat 'em and take his benz."

Then we heard the door open, and to our

surprise, it was Lisa and DJ Sno. We told him he was

about to get "dealt with," and we all laughed. We begin

to sing him our new song and told him about the car.

He said, "Yall always have something crazy going on."

He told us we could have the other room he got to

party in and said he would be back. He was good

people we trusted him.

He came through about 6:00 p.m., then we went

all around St. Louis. He pulled out a bag, handed Eve

"the stuff," and she rolled up a "joint." We all smoked

except for Lisa. Lisa didn't want me to smoke because

she knew I would get super relaxed. We were in an unfamiliar territory, but I needed to get my mind off of my troubles with the car. I wish I had never started smoking, because I liked the escape too much.

Weed helped me think in another dimension. It's like I could figure out everything and voices would give me insight where I had none. Yep, I needed to get in "my zone" to figure out my hustle plan in the music industry.

We went to the radio station 95.5 with DJ Sno. He knew everyone there and Tony let him say hello to the people. Then he introduced us to everyone. He also took us to East St. Louis where he grew up. I remember getting "the feel" of St. Louis. It reminded me of Milwaukee, dirty and ghetto, I liked it.

That Thursday we "hit up" a club called Tequila Wild on the landing. Murphy Lee, another rapper of the St. Lunatics, made a special appearance that night singing his world shaking verse off the remix of welcome to Atlanta. Lisa and I were on stage with him saying, "I thought I told ya, don't cross that bridge without permission from them St. Lunatics." I was "high as a kite" in the club. I remember looking at the whole crowd doing what the St. Louis girls called, "the stab a hoe" dance.

It was known to the world as the pancake. It was an outer body experience in that atmosphere. I was beginning to get use to getting that high from the atmosphere that celebrities created at a concert. Lisa and I and some other pretty girls were on stage as well.

Murphy finished a couple of songs as the women screamed and pushed towards the stage. When he left, we followed behind.

We were all going out the back door at the same time with DJ Sno. Lisa gave me the money purse because the club was filled with St. Louis drunk people. People starred at us as Murphy's bodyguard helped us down the stairs.

When we "hit the ground," it's like the crowd rushed us. We were being pushed by a force of people to the door. I felt my purse get really heavy, and I looked back only to see the security guard hand in our purse. I reached my hand in after his, and dug my long nails into his skin and twisted his arm. He blamed the crowd pushing him. I mugged him until we were safe outside.

The cold wind from the riverfront made my high of the weed and atmosphere come completely down. We were almost robbed in St. Louis our first night. They assumed we were with Murphy since we were on the stage together. I did not like the feeling and the pressure of being associated with celebrities.

St. Louis' people were envious of Nelly and the St. Lunatics. They wanted what they had, and would do anything to get it. If this is what really goes on behind closed doors because of the fame, I didn't want this, but I did want the excitement of being on stage from a high I couldn't get from a "blunt" or a drink. I am sure there was a way to taste the life, but not be affected by it…wasn't there?

That next night was Nelly's "Apple Bottom Party." I was determined to go, so I suggested we catch the train. Eve agreed to go with me, but Lisa thought it was crazy.

We caught the train to see the St. Louis "King." I was so excited that I was going on the Metro train, and I was not afraid of the late night gangster boys that might be on the train. I knew how to deal with "dope boys," it was like dealing with some of my family members. So when we were on the train, I looked them dead in the eye and I gave them the look like, "I wish you would." I told Eve what to do, how to survive in the city because Tulsa, where she lived, was so country. I told her don't smile, but you need a mean mug on your face. St. Louis people didn't understand kindness.

We exited the train and walked a block to the club. It was about 11:30 p.m. at night. I told her to walk fast. It was two women in "club clothes" at night. We were straight up on a mission this night. And we needed to make something happen at the club because the Metrolink stopped running and we were staying till after 3:00 a.m.

We went in the club and found a seat on the side. The atmosphere was exciting with a lot of the Rams football players there. I saw Chingy and his two brothers there as well. One of my favorite songs at the time came on. I heard, "Dip Set," "Dip Set," Dip Set" coming through the speakers as I made my way to the dance floor.

As I was dancing, I thought about last night as the security guard tried to rob us, and how I could feel the gangster in me come out as I heard Juelz Santana's voice. He was my other celebrity crush. I thought about his dimples and his down to earth, laid back personality. I liked those New York dude's' accent and style.

The room atmosphere shifted into admiration and homage as Nelly came in with Big B in front of him. I couldn't move my feet. I looked at him like I had seen a ghost. He was actually right in front of me. His eyes were beautiful and memorizing. I gave him a hug and a kiss on the cheek, and he politely said, "Thank you." He seemed tired, but grateful. He had a quick walk that allowed him to move swiftly through the crowd and up the stairs to the V.I.P suite.

This older guy that had been watching me all night came over and offered me a drink. However, it was distracting me from thinking of how I could talk to Nelly about the music business. He was just rambling on, then he called his nephew over to the table who was a Rams' player. The guy motioned for me to come follow him, and I did exactly what he said with Nelly in mind.

The security guard moved the red rope back as he admired my beauty. I didn't really know what to do in the V.I.P suite because it was my first time by myself. Also, I remembered the protocol from the Usher and

Snoop experience. I saw food, business people talking about deals, NFL football players, and really pretty ladies just sitting like dolls. I looked out from the second floor and saw people dancing downstairs; that looked like more fun. I turned around to see Nelly behind me talking to his friends. I said hi again and asked if I could take a picture with him. He said, "Yes, of course," and we posed for the picture. He said, "Thank you." He was so polite and humble, I thought, where was the guy from the videos? I grabbed his hand and he let me lead him away from his friends. We started talking, but I couldn't focus because his eyes took me into a different conversation. I could see right through him: he is so transparent. I saw a look that he really didn't want to be there, that he was just going through the motions. I gave him another kiss and he said, "Thank you."

I was ready to leave after I met the St. Louis "King." I left the V.I.P. suite and went back downstairs. I was ready to go. When I got back down stairs I meet some more men, then some more men. Drinks were "flowing" and so was the "high" of the music. I gave out my number and got all of the men's numbers I was interested in. Closing time of the club was a little blurry to me. I was good and tipsy not knowing how we were getting home. I had a choice of who I wanted to take us back to the hotel, but I knew this would be a set up for trouble.

As I laid in bed that night in the hotel room, in my mind, I ran through all the conversations that night

I had. If I was going to do this music thing, I wanted to promote someone I liked, someone I believed in, and someone I wanted to see win. Yep, I think Nellyville is where I wanted to be. I was definitely in Nellyville.

That next month, in December, I was at the "4sho4kids" fundraiser, which was one of Nelly's nonprofit organizations. I had contacted the office to see if they needed help with the company. Nelly's Auntie was over that department, so I spoke with her. The event was really nice and I met all the people who worked behind the scenes. It seemed like it was Nelly's family reunion because his mom, dad, sister, brother, uncle, aunts and cousins were there. I met Jackie and Mama Rhonda for the first time. Uncle Rick, Grandma Mack and everyone else. They were really genuine people. I could see exactly what a solid family he came from. I could tell Nelly was on his best behavior in front of his grandma. She was the sweetest woman I had ever met. There was a grace, peace and kindness that flowed from her that can't be bought. I loved them; they treated me like family. Yes, I wanted to work with these people. I wanted to promote a person who had a big heart. Nelly loved hard from what I saw. He would light up like a Christmas tree when the kids he helped came in the room. He knew them by name, and took the time to talk about their lives. I was impressed by his humility and how he honored people. His Dad, "Big Nell" had the same respect for people, too. It's in his bloodline, I thought, and that is when I decided I was all in. St. Louis became my new home.

Esther Jones

Chapter 3

DRINKING THE WHOLE BOTTLE

started out as an intern at Nelly's Inc. in 2004. I would go to the office everyday where I would see Kri, Tony, Quick, Chalena, Wootty and the others who were in and out working on various

projects. Some worked in the office others were on

tour or did shows. The music business was just that

busy. The partying and videos were only the tip of the

iceberg. It all started from an email or contract. The

department that I worked in was the "Pimp Juice",

Nelly's energy drink was called Pimp Juice. Everyone

wore multiple hats in the office. Most had to do a little

of everything to save time and money. I just listened

and learned, but didn't say much. The "Pimp Juice

parties" were lame to me. They really needed help, and

it catered more to the white college kids. I guess it was

selling there the most, but I saw a different approach.

I sent a proposal to Wootty about giving it to the

celebs in town and he equipped me with the products,

shirts, and things I needed. I just started going to every party, club, and event telling people about all that Nelly was doing. I was a fan of the music, so it was easy for me to promote him. He was wonderful in my eyes. I began to be known as Nelly's girl because I wore his brand: Apple Bottoms, his face, or Pimp Juice shirts at every event. I was also fun and the life of the party, so it was easy for me. I loved people and I liked having fun.

St. Louis was different from the six years of living in Tulsa, Ok. I didn't like Tulsa, there was only church prayer meetings going on there. I felt home in St. Louis; there was something for me to get into every day of the week: Gambling, strip clubs, nightclubs, day clubs, sex clubs, swinger clubs, river parties, car washes, celebrity parties, concerts or just people I met who had something going on at their house. I started to smoke

weed every day and just party, party, party! It was non-

stop action.

Chapter 4

INTOXICATED

B y 2005, I was only getting about four hours of sleep a night. I was still helping with Pimp Juice and networking with every celebrity or the people that came into the gateway city of the world – St. Louis. St. Louis was really on the map,

the radar from Nelly taking off everyone's clothes,

Chingy at the Holiday Inn Hotel, and rapper J-Kwon

"getting tipsy." I had just turned 21 and I had been to

every club nine times over. East St. Louis was my

favorite because it was easy to make money there. I

can't remember all the stars' name I met and

networked with, but it wasn't long before St. Louis

started to get boring to me. I was thirsty for national

stardom, not just regional. The force of the fame was

always pushing me to want more, to go higher up.

It was August 2005, in St. Louis. The Core DJs

worldwide invaded St. Louis. Mr. Milwaukee and his DJ

friends ran through St. Louis with a huge train that I felt

honored to ride on. I remember hearing about the

event in the local papers, St. Louis American and just knew it was for people like me. I didn't know at the time that the founder, Tony Neal, was from Milwaukee, WI. I went for networking and wanted to know why in the world would someone named their organization, "The Core." I would soon find out that weekend.

The vision of "The Core," DJs way of thinking made me change the way I did business from that day forward. The weekend of August 25-28th of the retreat changed my life in so many ways. It was also the time when Hurricane Katrina hit New Orleans.

I went to the Adam's Mark Hotel on that Thursday as usually to greet the people who were coming to St. Louis for the weekend. Networking is not just something I do naturally, but it's my passion.

Connecting this one with that one, linking up people that I knew needed to be linked up. It's just something in me who knows who needs to meet who in order to fulfill their purpose on earth. I went to the registration desk to meet the staff, and the team who was in charge that weekend. They were unpacking and setting up the T-Shirts, promo materials, and registration ready to check in.

I remember going to the bathroom where I ran into radio personalities D'Lyte and Cola. They had cool down to earth personalities that were like mine. I knew first off, they were no rookies and were in St. Louis for business. I was coming out of the bathroom and D'Lyte and Cola were going in. I handed Cola "an apple bottom card" because she had a beautiful face and a shape like a coke bottle. Perfect industry look for sure. They both were very welcoming and we talked a little business and exchanged numbers. They were doing video footage that weekend for their show. Everyone was on a hustling mission in St. Louis. I remember the electrifying atmosphere of all the different heads of states coming together. It was Chicago, New York, Dallas, Milwaukee, Houston, L.A, Detroit, North and South Carolina, Denver, Florida, along with Atlanta most influential people joining together. I also remember meeting DJs from all over, promoters and A &R's from record labels, I can't recall everything that happened because I was high and drunk all weekend.

That Thursday night was the "jump off" at club Plush. I went with D'Lyte and Cola, and we got there late. We came in and went directly to the stage where the Core was giving out the awards to Nelly and DJ MIX Master Ice. The crowd was "cool," and a lot of the music and entertainment industry people there. It was a feeling of honor and love in the room. I had never seen Nelly in such good spirits in the club like that night. I could tell he felt appreciated. I really admired the vision the Core had. It was much needed. Because no one really wanted to acknowledge the DJs, the producers, and the promoters who first believed in them or helped them in their music career. It really was an issue that needed to be addressed.

I remember talking to so many in St. Louis about why they hated Nelly so much. The answer never made since, all I heard was ENVY. I have told the local rappers and everyone coming up that when someone from your city "gets on," it automatically puts you on. They really didn't get it, they still hated him for no reason.

The music pulled me out of my painful thoughts and I started to dance. I remember all the heads of states mingling and looking for something to take home that night. I remember feeling, the burden to show people out of town a good time. The hospitality in me wanted to take them to the best clubs, strip clubs, restaurants, and sex parties they had ever experienced.

By now I was familiar with the way the industry really operated from the inside for women. It was the most eye opening two years' experience in my life. There are definitely two different worlds the stars live in. You have the private life and the public image. It is really like living a nightmare while living your long life dream at the same time. The nightmare is people having an opinion about what you drive; who you are dating? Your kids? Is that your real hair? Even from what brand of coffee you drink. I mean whose business is it why you do what you do? They are not God, are they?

You see, to some people who don't have a savior or know Jesus, they are their gods. Their lyrics in their songs help them through bad breakups. Their songs rescued them from suicide. Their songs made them work it out with their wives. Their lyrics comforted them through betrayals and gave them understanding of how the streets really think. The songs enlightened them, when they were getting played for a fool. So if

they could have that much control over the fans' life;

they have the right to voice their opinion of what they

should or shouldn't be doing! Or do they?

Chapter 5

ALCOHOL POISONING

I remember waking up on that Friday August 26th with the biggest hang over ever. What did we drink was my question?! Flashbacks of the party and then the after party at the strip club at "Bottoms Up" came to mind. I remember Cola and I getting told by the security to get down off the chairs because the paying men couldn't see the live porn going on, on stage. In the strip club the beautiful women don't get attention, but the fastest shaking booty does. It was cool with me, though, because it gave me time to count their money for them so they wouldn't miss the show.

That night my name made more buzz than just behind Nelly. The fact that I would always represent him harder than people who were originally from the Lou, I took care of the DJs, and I was a female hustler gave me mad cool points. That was what I did naturally, and people that recognized the gift will want you to work for them. Tony Neal was a boss and hustler by nature as well, so he could recognize this in people also.

The Core DJs brought the real behind the scenes hustlers together to teach people never forget who put you on or helped you. The Core gave people who had no one to believe in them hope. No one can do it alone in the music industry, no matter how they say they did. I was on the couch that morning at Catherine Jones' house reflecting on the night before. That's where I was staying because I started doing promotions full time. I couldn't afford to live in the house I had at first. I never liked apartments, so I just stayed there until I could save up some money. I met Stephanie, Nelly's cousin through Uncle Ricky Mack, which was Nelly's Uncle. Nelly's great Uncle on his mom side wife was

Catherine. Catherine Jones was such a sweetheart who was on hospice at the time. I loved the time I spent with her before she died; she had a sweet spirit.

I remember my phone ringing and it snapped me out of the flash back from the night before. I remember getting change for hundred dollar bills for so many men so they wouldn't lose their spot in the front row at the strip club. I had never been to an actual live porn scene like that. They were in the shower and any and everything went on that night. I don't even remember how I got home. I didn't like it, I loved it. I thought, I just found another way to make fast money. I knew a lot of pretty women who needed to be introduced to the strip club. I just needed a percentage and we could keep the money flowing in was my plan.

The Force Behind the Stars

The atmosphere and expectation was filled with fantasy and sexually pleasure. You could think of a fantasy and see it in action for the right price. However, I didn't like the fact that the women were being used as sex slaves, as sex objects auctioned off to the highest bidder. But the force behind me loved it -- exploiting women, while stripping them of their dignity and virtue was what it was after. To make them feel as though they are worth nothing but a big booty and good sex is what it degraded them to.

As 10:00 a.m. rolled around, I was dressed and ready to go again. This was the second night of the retreat and I already felt I had done too much. I entered the lobby of the Adam's Mark Hotel and was greeted by the echoes of "Star Jones" who "Star Jones" it was a word play Cola and D'Lyte made up from Mike Jones single that was out at the time. They were having lunch in the restaurant with a pretty girl named Fu Fu. I remember them talking about the latest celebrity news and I wondered off in my mind. I had no interest in the lives of the stars, I only like to talk about how they made money, their strategy concept.

Their private lives scared me, because some of them thought they were gods and could treat people like objects. Some had a cold evil heart of how they saw people who were "beneath" them or not famous. They would talk to people and not care about the person's' dignity or feelings. No respect for everyone, but just their circle of friends. To be honest an evil rapist with a Grammy is still an evil rapist to me. To the entertainment business; it's a different story. All they care about is the gifts and talents of the person, and the real them is being all used up. The fact that you have a gift of music that they could make money off of was all that the industry and industry professionals cared about.

I looked past all the fame, glamour, smoke screen and mirrors, and I look at their hearts, their words, and actions. Do they really care about others? I think I stood out in the industry because I wasn't a "yes man." I said exactly how I felt. If you were selling like crack on the music shelves; I still expected you to treat people right or you got reminded that the sun does not evolve around you. Most of them respected it because the people around them only said things to flatter their ego.

After my mind drifted back to the conversation, I heard the girls say we were leaving going to the awards show. I remember Fu being really funny and had straight forward and cool personality. I loved her from the moment I met her. The awards show was boring to me, because I liked to dance and party!!

The room was filled with industry professionals and executives and music moguls. G-Unit record label was there. Artist like from Young Buck, BMF, Yo-Yo, Tony Yayo and so many others. The DJs that started and carried the movements were in attendance too.

We networked, took pictures, exchanged business cards, and I handed out Pimp Juice to all the tables. I remember being tipsy from men congratulating my beauty with drinks. It was some fine rich men there, but I was very selective on who I had sex with. You couldn't be flashy or liked to show off. Those are the men that really needed a lot of attention.

Relationships in the industry are all about competition and what you got, rarely can you find one based on love. It's like they wanted you if all they boys said you were hot and if you were the hottest thing popping at the time. The men had a mindset that you were for them to show off. They didn't love you, because almost all the famous rappers I knew had a different females in each area code, but a main one they showed off with. There were the booty calls ones, the down ones who got their back in real life, and the ones they knew that was in love with their image and not them. When their image and money was down, then there went the chicks. They knew who really loved them or who was just holding them down, these were the ones that got treated the worst, though.

The women in the industry are no better though. Most women in the music industry only wanted a millionaire who would take care of them. They would get butt implants, breast implants to compete and be a good catch for the rich men they wanted. Honestly I talked to these rich men and the genuine ones that are really about love don't want a model chick. They want a submissive gentle wife that will not always be on the scene. The men wanted loyalty and not to be used for their status quo. I remember seeing pain and disappointment in the men's eyes who had experienced betrayal from people who they thought had their back. Only to find out when their music was no longer "hot" they got kicked out of certain circles. As well, the women who said they loved them kicked them out of their lives also. Both men and women just wanted someone who would never leave them or forsake them. They all wanted something real, but stuck trying to keep up with a superficial fantasy world. That's exactly what the entertainment industry is.

It's pretty hurtful what the men and women in the music industry have been through, but it didn't stop my pimping or hooking rappers up with girls. If they didn't know how the game went, then that's them, I got paid regardless. Yep, that life made my heart cold. I capitalized on ignorance and lust.

We took a lot of pictures and made silly videos that weekend. Fu and I clicked so well that we started hanging together. I knew it was deeper than music with her. She had morals and a deep respect of her friends rooted in her. I liked her straight from the heart approach and genuine heart. She was pretty and a hustler by nature which was awesome to me. We had to get dressed for the after party, so she told me to come with her.

She was a diva like Cola who had to change outfits every minute. I admired their fashion sense, but I wasn't really into fashion. After the beauty queen finally got ready, we left for the event at the club. She told me her story of how she broke two of her legs in a car accident, and had to take a break from the music industry. She told me of how everyone who she thought was for her turned their back on her. I thought about her stories and all the things I had seen, then I thought, "If this was the *"Good Life,"* then why does it hurt so much?"

We entered the club through the back door because the line was "crazy" long. It was not like a regular night; it was so many more industry people from all over the country who came to connect and party. We entered the club and went up on stage to the DJ booth where DJ Sno was on the One's and Two's. The thing I remember about that night is everyone had a place in the club and that our musical gifts came alive in those kinds of musical atmospheres. The gifts will

definitely manifest in those type of clubs climates.

If you were a worshiper, you would be the one

singing the words from the song to the sky or with

other people. Dancers are the ones who go into a

trance when they hear the beat, which takes them into

a place where they can release pressure or stress from

the day. Producers would hear the beats and generate

new ideas and concepts of songs. If your gift was a

rapper, you were making a remix of the song in your

mind. Then you have the watchers, who would sit back

and observe how everyone fit in as one.

The entire night we were in the DJ booth. As we

were in the booth, someone rolled up some weed and

we started a smoke session. Fu Fu and the guy I was

having sex with at that time was in the booth as well as with Dj Sno and a few of his friends. We smoked weed and drank free champagne all night. Free liquor was a rule for beautiful women in the club. It was an unspoken exchange that we let you admire our beauty as you pay with liquor.

I found out that the entertainment industry was all about exchanging favors. It's about giving a favor for a favor. In some cases, money can't get what you need done, but if you know a person in position that you have done a favor for before, it goes a long way. Definitely, I learned that everything was about giving and receiving favors. It is so much politics in it that it is not fair.

As I blew out the weed smoke, I realized no one really trusted anyone. Even those in the same group or ones who they called their partners still didn't know everything about them. There were so many secrets, lies, and secret sexually relationships going on that there was no trust. I thought, "What have I gotten myself into." Then I started to think about all the drama that was going on in St. Louis at the time with Chingy vs Nelly. I knew DJ Sno was still working with Chingy, because Chingy was "his people," and this is who he made money with.

I stayed in the DJ booth the whole night with my Pimp Juice cans on display. I knew first hand that Chingy felt some type of way about Nelly because one night on the Eastside at club Rio I offered Chingy a Pimp

Juice can and the bodyguard went into a rage, and cursed Nelly's name. I took a step back and stared at Chingy for confirmation. He put his head down like he was thinking about it, then took the Pimp Juice can. I always showed nothing but love to his camp and he knew this. I believe when you have so many other people involved with what is really been said, things get blown out of proportion. I knew this was what happened.

In the music industry, the gossip and people who hype up the story to make a rock a mountain are in it to keep drama going. The media often plays a part in allowing things to go too far and blow it out of proportion. I believe so many precious people would still be alive if it were not for, he said, she said whispers.

• • •

There have been so many incorrect stories that have never been told on who really caused all the drama behind some "beef." More than half the time, it is the members from the group or family that are offended that keeps the drama going.

Everyone who wants unity will have to kill their pride and admit a lot has gone on that they had no idea off wh. T really took place. The mature thing to do, is not react or let the social media know about it. You should always go to that person in person before . people, fans, and media get involved who don't even have anything to do with the situation at hand.

It created a lot of tension in St. Louis and a lot of sideline people saying if the "Derrty Ent" camp came in their neighborhoods, they were going to kill them. I definitely felt like I was in the middle because I had ties with people in Chingy's camp who I hung around with on a regular. I never really got to know Nelly or the St. Lunatics personally back then. Yes, I saw them at events, but it was just work. His family was my heart though, and I felt a loyalty to them for receiving me so freely.

The first house I ever spent the night at in St. Louis was Nelly's mom. When someone opens up their home, food, and their life to you, you should never forget that kind of love. I know I didn't. I knew Nelly from his family speaking on his character. He was more than a rapper to me; he was a great son, brother, dad, nephew and his love for children is what I saw in his big heart.

I heard the sounds of Trillville song, "Some Cut," that took me out of my confused world. We smoked a couple of more blunts of weed then it was time to head to the Eastside till day break.

That night was blurry to me and I had pictures that I don't remember taking, and I woke up in Fu Fu hotel's room. I don't remember how I got back to the hotel or even leaving the clubs. It didn't matter, though, I really did feel safe with Fu Fu. There are some people you can met one time and feel like you can trust them forever. This is how I felt with Fu Fu. I could trust her with my life.

The next morning I woke up, I had an awful headache, so I decided to smoke some weed to get rid of it. As I thought on the night before, I remembered getting offers to do promotions for so many other company brands. I remember people asking me why a lady from Milwaukee was representing Nelly so hard. I heard everything that night from people in my ear saying they were rapist, snitches, thieves, and haters. I never once believed it, but told them, it's "Derrty Ent." on mine.

They respected it, but hated me for my loyalty. I remember people who were on the "Derrty Ent" record label not wanting to be associated with Nelly's name in public or they did not want anyone to know they knew him. I remember the parties they threw where only 50 people showed up because of all the gossip. I never was a scary person who was easily moved by people's opinions, so I didn't let this deter me. I would put on "Apple Bottoms," request the "Tipdrill" song, and encourage the hating dudes' baby mama to dance to it, and throw up my middle finger to the crowd. People did like me because I was a party starter, but they also knew that I was honest about the whole situation. I was honest that it was petty and stupid, and that we could do nothing without unity.

That's why the Core DJ Retreat in St. Louis was special to me because I saw Tony honor both Nelly and Chingy in the time the drama was at its highest. He encouraged the city to recognize that Nelly took the "garage door off" for St. Louis to be heard, so everyone could run through it. He put the city on the map. Appreciation for Tony Neal and what the Core DJs did made me smile as I exhaled the smoke in the hotel room. It was a great moment in history when the Core DJs honored Nelly in St. Louis.

After the event, we went back to our room. Fu had to leave for the airport, so I walked her downstairs to the lobby; then I gave her a hug on the way out. I also told her to be careful because it was hurricane season. It was the day before hurricane Katrina hit New Orleans, which was one of the worst hurricanes in America.

On my way back up the elevator, I met a guy in the lobby. He was staring at me, so I said, "Hi." He smiled and said, "Whaddup wit it." I knew what that meant at 3:40 a.m. in the morning in a hotel. It meant want to have sex? I said something I am sure he did not expect. I asked him for a condom, but it was not to have sex with him, but to have sex with the guy I was having sex with at that time who was waiting upstairs in a different room for me.

He drilled me on why I needed a condom, so I drifted away in my head to find another source. Then a stripper looking lady was just coming down the stairs looking like she just got out of a sex party. I asked her for one, she gave it to me, and said, be safe. I wanted to give her my number to see if she ever needed some work to give me a call.

The alcohol had me wanting sex, so I was in a hurry, but later regretted not getting her number. I spent the night with the guy I was seeing at the time. I thought of all the conversations I had that night. These people hated me for loving and taking up for Nelly. I didn't see what the big deal was. They hated what I stood for. Then I closed my eyes in a bed with a man who didn't love me, confusion filled my mind. I thought, "What am I doing? I need to go to church in the morning."

It was Sunday night August 28, and I was still at the Adam's Mark Hotel with the people from the retreat watching the news about Hurricane Katrina. I suddenly felt small, I remembered in the Bible that this was one of the signs of Jesus' return earthquakes, chaos, wars, and storms. I wanted to pray, but the guilt from sinning held my tongue. I left and went home, and thought about New Orleans' tragedy.

After seeing all the devastating, craziest scenes on the news, I went to Church that Tuesday at the

Dream Center. They made an announcement that they were sending a team who wanted to go down and help the victims. I thought, "Man, I gotta go."

The next Monday I was on my way to Louisiana in a 15 passenger van with Joyce Meyers Ministries. I remember feeling helpless on the "Hurricane Katrina" trip. As I looked at the people in New Orleans, there was no peace or joy. They were losing their minds, and in a state of shock. They didn't need money; they needed peace.

I didn't have anything to give them because I didn't have peace myself. One night before we left, I knew I had to do what I was called to which was telling people about Jesus, because He was the ONLY God. He was the only real One people should worship, not these celebrities I was promoting. I knew in my heart this world stuff was only temporary and we will all die soon to either spend eternity in hell or heaven.

But I didn't have the guts to say anything. I kept Jesus a secret. I looked worn out and tired from the life I lived. I was depressed all the time and had to continually live in paranoia from being robbed. I had nightmares after my visit to New Orleans. I quit being a promoter and tried to stop my crazy living. I moved in with some prayer warriors from the church and worked at a daycare called "Happy Go Lucky" in North County.

I worked there for a little while, then at a different daycare, but I had no contentment. I didn't understand why people who didn't know Jesus or love

Him had so much money and lots of cars. I couldn't comprehend how I was living regular serving Jesus, but my old friends had fast money coming in and I didn't. I got offended at God. I was ashamed how I felt when I looked at the way God's people were living vs the world. Comparing the two worlds made me live in discontentment. I had peace that you can't buy, but I didn't have money like I liked it. I had no patience to wait on God to make me rich; I knew how to do that. I was done; God was to slow for me.

So in the summer of 2007, I decided to get back in promotions. I made some calls and I was on a plane to meet up with Fu Fu at the Core DJ Retreat in Dallas, TX. I knew I could get a job easy, everyone knew I was a pusher.

"Peace up A Town down" rang in my head on my way to Atlanta. The Dream, a R & B singer represented Atlanta well. He was showcasing his new single, "Shawty, You a ten." It was all Core DJs who have seen thousands of celebrities, so they were not impressed. He was nervous and His stage presence sucked to be honest. He did have a hit song though. It was my "jam," so I was dancing like I was his big cousin that always wanted him to sing. Everyone else was sitting down. The Dream felt me rocking with him so he came to the side I was on. Love is felt without words. I screamed really loud after the song was over. After the showcase he ran up to me and hugged me. I told him I didn't care if they wasn't feeling his song; it's a ladies hit, and if they played it, every girl in the club would dance. I told him it's about to be everywhere. He hugged me again and we took a picture. My word came to pass because it was everywhere the next month. I heard the song being played on the radios everywhere. The visions I had scared me, who was I for real. How did I just know who to give song to, to make it "blow up?"

That weekend, I finally got to met the guy that Fu Fu was dating, Luc Duc from the Iconz. We partied together the whole weekend. I wasn't officially with Nelly Inc. anymore, but the association has never been broken. In the music industry people always remember who you "came in under." I am grateful for Nelly letting me ride on "his coat tail," but after all the "hate and beef," it started up again with Huey, an up and coming rapper from St. Louis. But I was over the fighting and territory wars. I was not for drama anymore. There had been enough killings in St. Louis. I will never forget a conversation with the rapper, Irv Gotti that gave me so much clarity of why things were different with the St. Lunatics.

Ali, Murphy Lee, Kyjuan, of the St. Lunatics and the rapper Gipp were there, but Nelly was not. Irv Gotti was there in the room and so was the rapper Ja Rule, they are the coolest people ever. It was only a handful of people like them who were down to earth, not celebrity minded. They discussed the situation that went on with the Murder Inc. federal indictment. Ashanti, the artist from Murder Inc., the singer's behavior was discussed as well. It hit me all at once, I hadn't seen the connection between Nelly and this whole thing. Irv explained his issue with it being more than music with him, but He thought she was family. Ja Rule and all the Core DJs was talking about their views on loyalty. I was blown away with the truth. I saw the Tics, but something was different, something was missing. I thought about how talented they were and how Murphy Lee was never promoted like he should have been. This is when I started to see everything different. How could Nelly be riding with Ashanti and she did her people like that? When Irv needed her most; she "jumped ship." You can't just leave the people who "open the door for you" like that. We all have disagreements, but you can't ride in the good times while getting a Grammy, then get scared, and leave when things are going wrong. I needed some answers quickly.

Later that year in St. Louis, I heard that Ashanti was in town for a party. Jermaine Dupri, T. I were all in the Lou. I just wanted to know if the streets were right about what they said about Nelly. I wanted to know was it blinded loyalty or not. I wanted to know what the new St. Louis versus the Old St. Louis was all about. I wanted to know why Muphy Lee and Kyjuan were not at Nelly's parties or on his shows anymore. Why wasn't Murphy Lee, which had the bars was not supported and really backed up on Derrty Ent label.

I honestly thought Muphy Lee was a genius lyricist and never really got his chance. I could tell it was tension between the Tics and Nelly. They were together, but not together. Where was Nelly support when Murphy Lee needed him? Why was Huey people wanting to smoke with me? I wanted to know how I kept getting robbed? I would see Murphy Lee and Kyjuan at different parties than Nelly in the same night. Something was different, what did I miss while I was gone? I wanted to know after all this time was I just oblivious to what really was going on. I was in so much confusion and pain that I was drunk all day every day. I smoked more than I had ever had in my life. I just remember being in the V.I.P suite at the party with everyone upstairs and Nelly looking at me. He didn't speak or hug me as usually. He whispered something in "Big B," his body guard's ear and the next thing I knew I was being put out of the V.I.P suite. That was fine, the party was "wack" any way. I got pissed off when they took my cup though. That was so disrespectful.

I was so mad that I couldn't think straight. I went to the parking lot and waited for him to come to the truck. It takes a lot to get me upset, but once I do, I really can't calm down easy. He straight up ignored me and kept telling Ashanti something. At that very second; my heart broke. I didn't know what I did or why he couldn't face me. He had never done that before. I had never seen him with Ashanti either. I was "mugging" her because I had no respect for people who jump ship when it's sinking, but claim the people when they are winning. Was it the fact I personally knew a lot of the women he had besides her? I didn't know, but tears of betrayal fell from my eyes, and I wanted bloodshed.

In the parking lot I dialed the number of the people who had been telling me about how they hated him. I pressed the end call button. I knew they were for real killers, and just needed a reason. I thought of Nelly's mom, Rhonda, then I hung up. I cried some more on the way home, and smoked until I couldn't see, while Lil Boosie, "Set it off" played in the background. There was so much hate and drama I went through behind his name that people would never know. I was done with everybody then. I would only look out for me. The FORCE behind the stars had poisoned me and I started to hate people.

Chapter 6

THE POISON EFFECT

When a person has alcohol poisoning, they can become extremely confused, unresponsive, and disoriented. This was the condition of my heart doing this season in my life. It was poisoned. I felt betrayed, hurt and alone. I was making money still doing freelance promoting for local and regional artists, but I was a walking time bomb filled with bitterness and rage. I promoted whatever made money: women, models, sex, strippers, or porn stars. But I never got into selling drugs because I didn't want to end up in prison like my brothers. The fast money was cool from pimping, but I missed being with big name celebrities.

That feeling of being on stage is a drug. It's a high where you are happy with no worries. The only problem is that you are not on the stage 24 hours a day. When they got to the hotel room where there will be no more hand claps or the thousands screaming their name, they come down off that high. It's lonely, miserable and the facade comes off. When you see them in that state; it's miserable, and they are not good as their lyrics say they are.

I was listening to "Dying" by Lil Wayne on my way to Milwaukee, WI. I was going to link up with "Bone Thugs" n "Harmony". They happened to be in my hometown city and I needed to go home anyway the week they were there. I found out Tony, CEO of the Core Djs was home to; he was celebrating his birthday. He had an event going on with "Bizzie Bone" from the rap group Bone Thugs n Harmony, who at that time wasn't working with the group. He had a plan to get them together as a surprise at his event. I was for unity, so I called him when I arrived at the hotel. Everyone with them stayed at the same hotel. It was a smoke session going on in the bathroom and a wrestling match going on in the living room with Layzie and Wish when I entered their room. I gave the introduction of who Tony Neal was and they stepped out in the hall to talk business.

The talk ended with phone number exchanged and handshakes. I gave him a hug, and he was off to Miami to finish the celebration of His birthday.

It was about 4:00 a.m. and we were still partying. Layzie Bone said we should take the party out to the tour bus, so we all left. I first met him in person with Caine in St. Louis at the Crowne Plaza Downtown at the bar. That night in St. Louis I told them about a thing called the "Shindig" that happened every Sunday night. I called Mocha Latte', a genius promoter from St. Louis and I put Layzie Bone on the phone. Krayzie

Bone, the manager, the DJ and their bodyguards went with us too. We all left in trucks and followed each other. I texted a rapper named, Baby Boy Da Prince and we picked him up. He had a single called, "This is how I live" that was hot at the time, and he was pushing it in St. Louis. We partied, smoked, drank and danced all night.

I liked Layzie Bone, because of his down to earth personality. He was brutally honest, and was so welcoming. Everyone was drunk that night including the drivers. They smoked high grade of weed called "Kush" that I could only take one puff of. I was a rookie compared to these legends.

I don't remember what happened once we got to the club, but I do remember going down the hallways in the hotel bumping into the walls. I was higher than I had ever been in my life, and I couldn't walk straight or talk clear. I just remember running into the walls to try to get on the elevator. I thank Jesus for protecting me from getting raped or robbed in the hotel parking lot. I had come by myself and was too messed up to get home. I still don't remember what happened.

Obviously I hadn't embarrassed myself too much because in Milwaukee they embraced me once again. "Star, hit the blunt," Caine said in the bathroom. I said, "No thank you." I wasn't smoking no more with them. I could not "hang" on their level. I didn't want to black out again.

I was glad I got a chance to link back up with them. I really did like Layzie and we had a real heart to heart that night in Milwaukee on the tour bus. We talked about all the drama of groups splitting up and people leaving you when you are down. He told me about his children, his wife, and his love for all the people he hung with. I remember wanting to cry from some of the stories I heard. He was transparent about his mistakes, bad habits and times with Easy E, Snoop Dogg and Tupac.

I unbraided his hair as he fell asleep on my lap. I really admired him for his heart of gold. He was indeed a good, loyal friend who was a peacemaker at heart. Our conversation made me think about all the stories I heard from many celebrities that had had their hearts broken, been a part of betrayal and robbery schemes, diamonds stolen from them, been robbed for their cars and so on. I was convinced this was not the good life; it was the definition of the deception of riches. It didn't produce what it said it would. We were still depressed, suicidal and isolated in that world. No matter if you just lost you mama or baby brother, the only thing the label wanted to know is where is the money? All the managers just wanted to pimp you for your gift. It was just a big prostitution game. You can exchange more than sex. You can sell you, your freedom, your gift, your honesty, your value, your virtue and the truth. And by now, I was tired of being used. I was tired of pimping and being pimped. I had no peace, I couldn't sleep, and the nightmares were back.

Contrary to popular belief, Jesus wasn't walking with us in the strip clubs, dance clubs, and concerts that promoted everything He hated: lying, pride, drunkenness, worship of man, having sex with people we were not married too or doing drugs was sin. You can't have double standards and only pray when your family is sick, or call on Jesus when you are getting robbed or shot at. Yes, I wanted to serve Jesus, but the love of money sat on the throne of my heart. I wanted to make my name great. I wanted to be known, but not to face the truth that I craved the worship of man, and didn't want to worship Jesus. This was definitely "Egypt" – the place of deception and bondage. We were slaves to the fans and slaves to our sins; this is what we were controlled by. We were slaves to the FORCE behind the stars. We were just that...slaves.

Five years in the music industry was like being on a roller coaster ride, and I got the whole idea of the behind the scenes politics. In like most male dominated industries, there were a lot of womanizers. I meet so many womanizers and pimps who used titles such as managers, DJs, or CEO's to cover their true identity. They knew me from one time meeting me. They knew I was too strong to be pimped by them and to sell dope. The role they saw me fit was promoting, networking, recruiting women, and giving them whatever they needed to make the business work. But this poison had me slowly dying.

The Force Behind the Stars

I looked old and worn out in my face, and my mind was a nervous wreck. I was truly dying! I was not the innocent, naive 19 year old girl anymore as I was when I first came into this industry. A part of me died with every hustle, every lie, every trick, and every one night stand. In that world women had sex with women, and the rappers encouraged them to do it. They would pay money to see them have sex parties. It was all just giving your body whatever it wanted. We were selfish monsters. It was not living. I was dying and getting deeper in the trap of each addiction every day.

This poison made me delusional in order to live in this imaginary world where money, drugs, sex, and fame seemed like the best thing ever. I didn't like to be sober because I would think of all the lives I was messing up. I thought about how I didn't' talk to my family or how I never saw my nieces and nephews. I hated the person who I became, but I couldn't break free from what I had gotten myself into.

I remember watching famous rappers who were treated as gods on stage, but behind closed doors, they were verbally and physically abusive. I remember telling one that he needed anger management because if you got upset every time something doesn't go your way, you will be fighting your whole life, but his anger and frustration grew. There was a monster that came out of these celebrities and industry professionals after every hand appeasing show. The fans, the worshipers who didn't know him off stage loved him. They would never see the dark side of these rappers. There was indeed evil, hateful, hurtful, and murder was lying dormant in their soul.

In this rapper's hotel room that night; he was hitting a white line with a hundred dollar bill rolled up. Offering cocaine to someone was common as asking someone if they wanted water. I remember looking into an arena full of people waving their hand to this image, not knowing the evil demons some of them really have become.

Just like with the alcohol effect, you feel horrible the morning after, but you still want to drink again. You need it to drown out the fact, you miss spending time with your children. The demand of the force makes you sacrifice everything that means something to you. You try to stay drunk to avoid the fact that your inner circle was one decision away from leaving and betraying you.

I would see the three or four women go in the hotel room of a married celebrity who claimed they were faithful on camera. I would watch as the money kept secret lovers tongue quiet from decades of adulterous relationships. The men who walked in stardom power convinced the side chicks they were lucky to have them at all. I remember having talks with beautiful women with low self-esteem who was tired of the creeping and the hiding, but did not want to give up the "hush" money. The frustration from the force that caused swollen eyes, busted lips and trips to the abortion clinic like it was the corner store is normal in this type of life.

The Force Behind the Stars

If you choose the life of the rich and famous, you choose to put up with the drama that comes with it. The women are accustomed to sharing their men. I had a part in all of this. I thought, how could I still be a part of this? It was severely corrupted. I would meet their wives, then side chicks later in the hotel room, then the groupie one night after the concert who lined up just waiting for when they were called next.

I couldn't really speak on how I knew this was not right, because the fruits of my life agreed with it. You see, I called myself being loyal to the famous rappers whose lies I told. It's funny, the same ones I see on television saying they are the truth, are the ones who lie the most. Now that I look back; it was the works of Satan. He can twist and manipulate thousands, then cause them to spread the lies so everyone thinks they know the truth, but it's all a web of deception. Yes, we all had the same spirit of whoredom and mammon. We all agreed that because of who we were, the people should be honored to serve us. It was vanity at its highest level.

I remember my first years in the music industry and being hurt by rejection from what I wore, what my hair looked like, or what I drove. I remember the women who were around Nelly in a club looking me up and down with an "I'm better than you look" because of their Lui or Gucci bag. I have seen Fendi make women walk more confident as the aroma of vanity filled the air. I remember them saying with their eyes, "What did the celebrities see in me? Why were they cool with me? I didn't fit in their box of the industry check list." I wasn't rude or mean. I would speak to the bartender as well as the valet parking guy. I had a flashback down memory lane from outside the club where one of Nelly's women just interrupted the conversation we were having and stood right in front of me to block him from seeing me. He saw the rudeness and took care of it smoothly.

These women didn't know me, but hated me. I remember being hurt deep from women in the music industry who were defined by who they had sex with, what magazine cover they were in, who's latest video they were twerking their butts in, and by who had the biggest booty.

I never thought like that about myself. It wasn't my style to brag about who I knew, or where I shopped, or who I was sleeping with. I was about getting money, but not really bragging about it. But the revelation hit me in Milwaukee when the liquor settled in. I was vengeful from the treatment from women, so I sold them to the men. I was the woman who started off in the music industry getting known by NOT sleeping with all the rappers, Djs, or Record Executives. I could out think most of the professionals in the industry who called all the shots. It was my intelligence and business mind they envied. Most of the other women, they just had sex with them, so they were jealous because they never were invited to discuss business.

I saw the envy and hate from the favor and treatment I got from celebrities, but not having to have sex with them "to be in the room." I remember right before a beautiful chick went into a room of 10 guys to please them; she had a look of sorrow mixed with regret and asked me why I wasn't forced to do what they wanted. Why was it that she was being pimped out, but not me? Why did she always have to give her body to be used, and I replied to her, "The world is filled with pimps and hoes, you are or you just are not."

I honestly got started learning to hustle women early from my big brothers. I was able to think independently, without an entourage or a man over me. Women with strong men in their lives can run with the big boys. My dad was a truck driver, pool playing, juke-joint player, a "jack of all trades." Now, my mom, she didn't have any "game;" she just knew Jesus. My daddy taught her about those kind of men, and raising my brothers taught her how you can get hustled in 10 seconds in the Jones house.

I was the youngest of all 15, and I took in every lesson from all my relatives. I learned about Jesus and loved Him, but the influence from my brothers taught me to eat or be eaten. I would say my big brother, James Jones, taught me the toughness I have. He would force me to fight him back when he punched me. I was a peacemaker at heart, but he wanted me to know how to kick butt if someone messed with me. I had a love and care for people he didn't have. He thought everyone was out to get him, and that everyone was his enemy. It was the way young black men thought all over. He was bad like Bart Simpson, off The Simpsons television program, and I was smart and a "goody two shoes" like Lisa Simpson. When I got into the music industry the influence of Bart went into full effect. Pimping and hustling was just in our bloodline.

In reality, all of the people in the music industry were forced hoes. We didn't have a choice when it pulled on us, we had to obey. There is a dimension of darkness where it can be so familiar that if you couldn't get a release here, you would miss it. You would miss the familiarity of the hurt, the hype of the drama, its pain, but it was twisted in our minds as companionship. You would feel alone and bored if a lot was not going on as usual. As demonic as it was, we felt that the demons of greed, and the demonic wisdom that counseled us was our friends and companions. We needed to get in that zone, in that place that everything in our world made sense. There was a lot of the logic, belief system, and a theory behind our actions. It made no sense at all, but in our minds; it justified our cruel behavior.

As I watched him sleep, I thought what have I gotten myself into? What type of monster had I become? I hated seeing the women pimped and picked out in the club like cattle for the slaughter of their dignity. We would go to strip clubs and the celebrity god would pick three or four women who they wanted to see fulfill their fantasy. That's when I would make it happen. I would tell them what they wanted to hear --

that they were beautiful -- invite them to the V.I.P

suite, make them feel wanted and included in our

group that the rest of the world envied. They took the

bait every time. They would be pretty women, but the

fantasy we sold them was that this life was the best

thing going, but in reality it was torment and sorrow

paved in gold.

The snoring of the celebrity laying on my lap

interrupted my regretful thoughts. I started to get

sleepy also. I looked around at the beautiful tour bus,

then I thought about how my journey first got started.

The words, "I was ugly" was definitely proven wrong by

now. I was living my "prove the haters" wrong dream,

but I still wasn't content; I still wasn't satisfied. The

deep longing to be loved and accepted still haunted

me. I was still empty inside. I tried to fill it with drugs, sex, lots of sex, but it never was fulfilling. It was a deficiency deep from my childhood that had not been filled. It was deficiency in a lot of the celebrities and rappers' souls, too.

Extreme extravagance is what happens when you are trying to fill a deficiency. That's why they wore four chains that their necks couldn't hold. They wore clothes that were extremely noticeable like a pink elephant. We all had deep voids that we were trying to fill with material stuff, fame or power. It was a never ending cycle of disappointments.

The cycle of disappointments came from us being the person everyone wanted us to be, but still being rejected. The hurt came from trying to please everyone to be accepted. Our hearts grew cold from being who they wanted us to be, and still not being accepted. Then you are just like forget everyone who don't accept us phases.

Our feelings were numb, and our hearts were cold. I would see grown men not know who they truly were. They would start off as a sweet innocent person, but take on this false identity. Most celebrities are in an identity crisis. I would be Esther at my house by myself, but then "Starr Jonez" at the club. I would hate having people expect me to act how they wanted me to act. They made us performance-oriented. We had to perform to be accepted. Whose attention and affirmation were we striving to gain? They had a deep sense of inadequacy and insignificance if their single was not on the top of the charts. The industry didn't

recognize us unless we did something worth praising.

The mentality of how the industry is set is based off

competition and being the best. In actuality, after the

bright lights went off, when they are out of their top

dollar brand of clothes, once they are out of their

Lamborghinis cars, and without the fans screaming

their name, THEY FELT WORTHLESS. The fame drug was

coming down, and the only place they felt like

somebody was only on the stage. They needed that

place of affirmation of this false identity they created

and their souls craved for it.

Most rap, sing, dance, strip, or become a DJ to

get someone to love them and accept them for them.

The force made us feel like we were not good enough

to be loved, so we always were on a mission to prove that we were worthy of being loved. We would use our gifts to be accepted and wanted around. If you ever dealt with a famous rapper/singer who can't perform, then you have seen the depressed, horrible black hole they sink in. I saw them hate the person they became, but when the lights come on stage, they transform into that alter ego state -- just to be normal and accepted is their heart's cry.

It's because we felt like we always had to do for people. There were so many demands put on me to be who I was not. I would have to perform, act, and be something I wasn't really inside. I started off being an innocent, naïve Jesus loving young lady, who loved people. But over time, this industry made me bury who

I truly was. I was kind at heart, but everyone told me I needed to be mean. It forced an image on me I wasn't. We were all bipolar. We were two different people, who went by two different names. And the drugs, liquor and sex is how we tried to drown out the confusion of our identity.

I don't want to make it seem like I never partook in the many sex escapades in the industry, because I did. I loved smoking weed. I loved getting drunk. The bottom line was, I needed love, which caused me to have multiple sex partners as the result. You see, the force caused the void to never be filled, satisfied, and never full. You first want just one loyal sex partner, then three in the Jacuzzi, then five who go both ways. Then the more drugs you have, the more pills you pop.

You create an addition to get a greater high than you did the last time. Sex partners were with rich strangers or anyone who loved sex in our group as much as you did. It's just one big orgy in the music industry.

The thing with the force is as I continued to feed it; it demanded more. It never produced happiness, but temporary thrills. Even after I obeyed the demons, it didn't meet my need to be understood or my need to be embraced, but it only used me up. I wanted to be known for me. I wanted to meet genuine people who cared for Esther, not just interested in how I could give them the connection. Were there any people with no strings attached? I guess I couldn't ask for something I wasn't. I went in cycles to fill this void, which left me with STD's, guilt, shame, and no virtue or worth at all. I just wanted to prove my haters wrong, to make money, to be successful, but now I was in way over my head.

I had contracted several STD's, and I remember one time having four at one time. The thing about drugs and drunk people is that we live for the moment. Condoms were a hit and miss. These were people with money, in the industry, who didn't look like they had a disease. I knew it was nothing but Jesus' mercy that I never contracted the HIV virus.

I always seem to put myself in life threatening situations. I remember leaving the strip club on the east side with two females. I didn't remember where my car was or how I ended up riding with them. They were both in the front and I was in the back seat. Suddenly the car pulled over and a lady got out the passenger side and got in the back with me. I looked out the window and saw trees with darkness all around. It was 4:00 a.m. on the eastside; I couldn't jump out the car. What was going on? She said she wanted me and started to kiss me. I laughed nervously, but I really was contemplating on throwing her head against the window. She kept grabbing at my pants while I refused her by pushing her hand away. I guess they thought I was too drunk to fight. The other girl got out and got in on the other side blocking me in. I thought if they think I was going to let them rape me, they had another thing coming. I said a prayer in my head that if Jesus would get me out of this without me going to prison, I would give up this life.

They finally stopped touching on me, and started feeling on each other. They said, "Star, you're no fun!" She got back in the driver's seat and headed to St. Louis. I saw the arch and exhaled. When I got in my door, I cried. I was tired of the rapist, the monsters, the cruel heartless rappers, and tired of men trying to control me with money. I was tired of selling chicks like CDs, and I was tired of not having a conscience anymore. The force behind the stars had me by the throat. Spirits of perversion and prostitution choked me to obey them. I wanted to quit; I looked old and tired. If Jesus was real, I couldn't hear his voice anymore. I was owned by the force.

I remember being at a New Year's Eve party and I was upstairs in a V.I.P suite sleep. I went from a friendly, fun, party girl to a hustler with no compassion. When Lil Wayne raps about an icebox where his heart used to be, I could understand. We all listened to songs; we could relate to. I hated the music industry. I hated what it did to me. I hated how it mocked Jesus and all He stood for. Jesus teaches us to love your enemies and forgive. The industry and hip hop teaches us to f**k you, hate you, unless you making money for and with them. It told us you only live once, so live it up. It told us money is everything, and once you get money and fame, you will be happy.

It is all deception! It was glitter, glamour, fame all wrapped up in death. It deceived us into thinking once we got all the things that the video showed us, we could finally have peace. It lied to us, there was no peace or joy. The top is the loneliest place because of the envy and torment of having to keep it. Every song screamed to me that people would love you and you would be popular. Those same people who ate with you would switch sides on you, killing you was the reality of the music industry.

I woke up at the countdown on New Year's Eve after I had passed out from two weeks of no sleep. I started to go on stage as usually were the celebrities were as I heard Pimp C song playing in the background. He had just died and there was a grief in the industry because of it. The atmosphere shifted as the Baton Rouge rapper, Lil Boosie's "Wipe Me Down" song came on and everyone started going into the same dance in one accord. I just looked at the whole crowd moving and releasing worship into the air. You see, every time you sing a song; you release what you are singing into the atmosphere. You have communion and fellowship with as well as entertained that deity that created it.

The atmosphere would shift from anger and murder when the DJ played "9mm" and we all yelled out the lyrics. I remember a rapper named Akon on the hook telling us not to cross that line creating an intensity in the air. I would see two people mugging each other, but if a R Kelly song played, the atmosphere would shift to wanting sex and not wanting to fight. The music created the atmosphere for what was about to happen. Slow R & B songs got people in the mood for sex, not war.

Lust would fill up people's mind as they thought about how they were going to take a chick home afterward. It is definitely bigger than a person or image, and it been this way for some time. It's a sound that the force must release to get its purpose done in the earth. In certain atmospheres, it is easier for certain things to happen. The music controls the atmosphere.

I remember sleeping being awakened by one of my sex buddies who danced repetitively in the mirror with a gun to a hateful song talking about killing his haters. Once the beat began, the rhythm came into our bodies. We would go into a uncontrollable trance. I would wake up at night with demonic spirits over me suffocating me to where I couldn't move. I would be paralyzed and could only think the name of Jesus, but not say it. I was tired of sex demons driving me to

different men. I was tired of the life, but I needed the

money and I could understand also how I could ever

live a normal life.

Chapter 7

OVERDOSE

I remember being in a hotel pool in August at a concert in St. Louis thinking how do rappers survive when they have no hit songs or shows to get income from. They have that money come in, and get accustomed to it, but then a serious shift takes place to where they are on the bottom. No one likes

---

the music or buying their single. The phone is not ringing for shows, and it's the most depressing thing ever to an artist who once was hot. To be known, then no one cares who you are is a pain that hits deep in your soul with rejection. What would they do to live now? When you lived off the music industry for 10 years then you don't have that support, you go into fear, into panic. It's every celebrity's worst nightmare to lose it all. I started to see the game in 3D vision. Where how the force will trap them and force them to live a lifestyle they couldn't really afford to live. If you only had one hit song, then years down the road, your money will start looking funny. That's why you see sometimes rappers filing for bankruptcy and owning back taxes because of the undisciplined lifestyle they were living. They go from the trap from the ghetto to the trap of the force. It was all an image that they felt pressured to keep up with. This "hit" me like the cold water I was in at the hotel. They are trapped by their own image the people created for them. Then they signed on with record labels that speak of their purpose like Death Row did with Tupac.

It amazes me that they didn't understand the power of words that were spoken over them and over the people. I would think, when are you going to grow up? You still are talking about how you love the trap, but haven't been in the hood in 10 years. You moved as soon as you got the money. It's a cycle because you encourage this next generation to do the street life in your music. You tell them, it's tight, it's hot, it made you rich, but the truth is all your close friends are dead and gone. To speak of murder in you music and promote that kind of rap is destruction. You claim the white people or cops are killing us and yell, "Hands up, don't shoot" at the officer who gunned down Mike Brown, but your music is gunning down our people.

I remember the rappers who claim to bosses and in control, but are controlled by record contracts, deadlines, and blood covenants. To have to keep up with this false image is a trap. It is so much drama, betrayal, and restrictions that go on behind a record deal. It's every artist's dream at first to get a deal, find people who will be your family and see your vision of where you want your music to go. Every artist wants to find a people who will hear their soul through their music. The industry plays on the game of the hopes that the artist has for being heard. They see a rapper who is young, ignorant of the system and ready to do anything to be known, to be famous. I have seen them come in with an original style, then the industry conforms them to an image they want. It forces them to only sing or rap about killing, selling dope to their black community, which degrade your people. It's just like the traps in the ghetto. The ones affected by the action in the trap is the person's community; their "own" people is who they are annihilating. I used to watch them make tens of millions from selling out. They may have 1,000 songs, but only 12 get picked by the A & R of records label only want these to go out. It's all about what the big man wants to be put out. The force only wants what will destroy this generation to be released.

The artist know they are a slave to the system, but they go on with it instead of realizing they bring the talent, the gift. If they would all come together and refuse to do degrading, killing, gangster music, it would force the industry to accept art that is positive.

The majority of the rap artist and R&B stars come from a life of being rejected. Like I said before, their original identity may have been quiet and peaceful, then they are called a punk, if they are too quiet or boring by people who don't understand who they are. After years of rejection by people who are supposed to receive you and accept you, you start to reject who you are. When you reject who you are because you are not embraced, then you look to the streets, the hood, or a group of people that will welcome you and include you in their gang. The only thing is you can't fit in that clique either, unless you become who they want you to become. When you have been left out and rejected, you take on this FALSE IDENTITY. You become who you know they will accept.

I would spend time with these celebrity stars who are very quiet and well mannered. Once they get around people from the industry, then there comes the pressure to change into this false identity they have took on. I see them transform on stage and act like a straight animal. Who are you for real was my question? What a torment to be living for acceptance of people, to be living for the hand claps. Yes, it's all about this "force" agenda, for people to be something they are not. On the other hand, it's the R&B stars and rappers who are evil and are woman beaters. Sometimes they will slap women in a minute and then force them to do sexual acts with his whole group, but get on stage and sing about how he loves women. WHAT??! Yep, they all have false identities, even the people behind the scenes. We all took on an image, an identity we hated. In the core of our being we were not who we pretended to be. Our identity was rooted in what the crowds thought. It was such a fear of abandonment, a false facade we put up, because we might not be accepted.

I was at a concert of a rapper named Juvenile once on the east side of St. Louis. This club is known for killings, shootings, and murders. All the men had a "burner", a gun on them and a blunt in their hand. I looked around and saw the hate and animosity in the room. The whole trap from different neighborhoods were there mugging their enemies down as Lil Webbie's "What's Happening" was released through the speakers. I heard the hateful hostile lyrics bring people into an atmosphere full of wrath. Juvenile entered the club from the back, and people started pushing toward the front. I saw him sing the Nola clap song, as New Orleans and East St. Louis shook hands in the spirit. He gave homage to the east side saying how he had ties with the streets there. It all made sense to me at that point.

You see the force behind the stars has his people set up all over. Have you ever seen the connection where a song is released and certain people governed by that same spirit love the song? You see, East St. Louis and New Orleans wards were full of bitterness, hate, false identities, gangsters, poverty, greed, prostitution, murder, and desperation. When Juvie released his song, they already knew the lyrics. The whole club became one choir in unity singing, "Slow Motion," the hypnotizing beat backed by the stripper influenced song caused women to dance like strippers. I watched as the beat for "Set It Off" start, which provoked anger to rise up in the club as people exhaled the smoke. It was as the demonic spirits in the people had one agenda, kill the humans. I saw people point guns at each other, then after the event, they did

not know what had happened. It was all spiritual, all a

set up by a deity that required blood from them to go

up in a higher rank. There was always someone dying

after a concert in the parking lot or at the show. Were

these murderers just random? No, I would say they

were sacrifices that are required in the blood banks in

the heavens from these principalities that they are

ruled by.

Just as the cold water hit me and woke up my

body, so did the revelation of how we had been

bamboozled by the force. I started to miss Jesus at that

very moment.

I missed His presence, the joy and peace He gave

me. I missed his safety, His comforting words through

the Bible. I missed true joy, not just happiness from a moment with drugs, sex, a good orgasm, or fat contract. I missed Him loving me for me. I never have to pretend with Him or keep up the false image of "Star Jones." I could be Esther. I didn't want to be paranoid. I wanted to sleep without images of me dying and my people being murdered running through my mind. I was tired and I wanted out. I knew I would miss getting my hair done every three days and shopping anytime I wanted, and I would definitely hate cutting myself off from the people I had formed ties with....BUT I wanted to go home. I was ready to live for Jesus, not the force. I wouldn't know how I would survive or make money, but I was not about this life anymore. It was the highway to a slow death.

The Force Behind the Stars

I got the revelation in the swimming pool of what I had really gotten myself into. Eve had come down for the weekend and we were at the hotel where the concert was. It was Sunday around five and I was already drunk. The concert started at 6pm as local acts opened up for the headliner who was Murphy Lee of the St. Lunatics. I was watching the concert from the balcony of our room. It was Murphy Lee's time to go on stage and I wanted to get a closer seat, because he had always given a good show. The crowd had always participated well with Murphy Lee and was very interactive. I remember when I first met Murphy Lee at a benefit concert for the children at a place called the pageant. Nelly and the St. Lunatics were always doing so much for their city, so I really never understood why people from there hated them so much. The kids yelled out, "L.O.V.E me" as Murphy instructed them to sign along. The room was packed out and it was a fun, positive environment. He came to the side I was at and bent down to say his rhymes like he usually does and a kid grabbed his arm. The kid couldn't have been more than eight years old. When the star struck kid grabbed his arm, Murphy's diamond bracelet ripped off as well. I remember Murphy pointing to who had it while still rapping the verse. The bodyguard was on the way to the kid who was in shock with a Murphy Lee's poster gripped in his hands. I was only steps away as I saw a small girl pick up the bracelet he snatched off. She returned the diamond bracelet to Murphy Lee and he rewarded her with all the cash in his right pocket. I saw her scream and I told her to put it up and go home with all the money. I have admired Murphy Lee ever since that experience. He is a gentleman with good manners.

Murphy had finished his verse and I made my way back to the hotel room. I was tired from a weekend of no sleep. Eve came down with her friends Jazz and Jazzy who were kicking it like it was New Year's Eve. There was so much liquor for everyone to get drunk three times. We were not the only one with rooms there, because as I walked down the hall, I saw most of St. Louis' people there, in the spot that night. It was late and Eve decided to go to the Waffle House to take care of the "munchies" that usually occurs after smoking marijuana. . That night, I had smoked a lot of weed, so eventually I passed out in the room. I don't remember how long I was sleep, but I will never forget what woke

me up.

Chapter 8

Getting Out

Bang! Bang! Bang! As gun shots rang out in the lobby of the hotel, a fearful crowd cleared the lobby. I jumped out of the chair I had fallen asleep in, and my feet automatically ran to the sound where I heard the shots. I came to a body circled with people just staring at him dying. I went into instant reflex mode and fell to my knees and began to do CPR on him. I went for about 10 rounds until, I was exhausted. He finally exhaled and started to breath. The circle that surrounded him let out a sigh of relief as his close friend called his name. I whispered into his ear for him to call on the Lord Jesus and he would be saved. I told him about Jesus, then I finally realized I was on my knees in a puddle of blood. I didn't know he was shot, I thought he just passed out.

The police arrived to put yellow tape around the crime scene. They were looking for the shooter. I touched his chest with a knowing, he was not going to make it. The ambulance took over and he took one last breathe. I cried tears of regret because He was just at the concert partying. I hope He knew Jesus is what I thought. I was sober like I had never been before. I was sober about what this life was really all about. The ambulance just sat their messing with their tools ignoring the victim, so the crowd started yelling for them to do something.

They rolled the lifeless body out on the stretcher to be put in the ambulance truck. They all gathered in a circle to pray, and I was thinking what's wrong with us? We pray after our sins get us in trouble. It was too late for prayer, he was dead and we were dying, too. I knew life. I knew Jesus. And I knew he was the way, the Truth and the Life. They may have never experienced joy, but I knew better. I always knew the truth through all the people I saw shot and killed. I knew the truth about what life was really about. I knew the truth about why we really are on earth. I knew that demons were real, and there was a real hell. I knew there was a real God named Jesus that died for them and they didn't have to go to hell if they accepted what He did and let him be Lord of their lives. I had a lot of blood on my hands for my influence that I had in some of these bad situations. I know a lot of people would have went a different way if I would had told them the truth. The influence of my voice was powerful and strong. I was done with this foolishness. I was done partying, sexing, drinking, and hanging with people who worshiped themselves. Self-worship leads to destruction and vanity. Humans were never meant to be worshipped. These celebrities were false gods who were human just like me. They don't have a heaven or hell to put me in, so why should I serve or worship something as flesh and blood.....human.

I was done and my eyes were being open to the deceitfulness of riches. I read the story about Jesus and how He was tempted by the devil to fall down and worship him and if He did, he would give him any and everything. That's exactly what he is offering now. Satan wants his place back as Lucifer. He wants to be God. He wants our worship. Humans are just pawns to him. He is a deity that craves worship, service, admiration, loyalty, obedience and homage. That's why we as humans, must understand that our worship is precious; it's everything. The Lord Jesus is looking for loyal worshipers and followers who won't bow down to Baal worship.

The thoughts of regret flooded my mind the next months as I made plans to leave St. Louis. I had gotten word that a guy associated with Derry Ent had shot him. I had always seen him around that team, but never knew that a murder would happen. He lost his life over a dice game, over money and ego. I went back into the hotel room, got in the shower and cried. I thought about all the bloodshed over dead presidents and over money. I thought about how the love of money can turn people against each other. I saw people who were friends, who hung out together, and did all sorts of things together, fight and kill each other over greed.

I have seen the demonic spirit of envy in people who were in Nelly's camp riding with him and hating him at the same time. I never did find out what really happened or got closure with Nelly or my old associates, I just left. I wanted to tell Nelly, thank you for all he had done for St. Louis, for me, and for the people who never will say thank you. He let me represent him and he always has respected me. I wanted to tell him, I thought he was an amazing man, with a heart of gold. I always saw him as a leader, and I knew what he longed for and the acceptance he craved for could only come from Jesus' love. I wanted to tell him Jesus could heal all his childhood abandonment issues. He always accepted me and favored me. He was always happy to see me, and the feeling was mutual. I wanted to get an understanding about what happened that night at the party with Ashanti. I knew in my heart that he wasn't what I heard people told me; I saw him different. I had no understanding, and after the murder, I didn't really care for any of the drama that came along with it. I was tired of the music industry ruling over me. In the music industry, the people didn't know what love meant. They couldn't see they were pawns to the force behind the stars. But they knew deep down if they couldn't rap anymore, they would be forgotten. They knew if they couldn't DJ anymore, no one would call their phone. The club owners knew if their club was gone, the fine, young, women would be gone, too. They knew if they didn't work at the radio station anymore, they wouldn't be needed. They knew people didn't love them, but their gifts. They thought the ache they had in their soul to be loved would be healed through people applauds. There is the love of man, then the love of Jesus. I knew that love of Jesus, and I had tasted the goodness of the Lord. I knew the rest was all hype, and I was out.

The pride of life, lust of my flesh, and the lust of my eyes pulled the cords that ruled my life. I couldn't get out of it if I wanted to. I had to cry out to something bigger, stronger, more powerful and wiser than the force. His name was, is, and will always be Jesus! He broke the tight grip it had on me. It happened at a church called Metro Christian Worship Center in St. Louis, MO. I will never forget a prophet of God named

Raphael Green who God use to speak a word through that made all the hell over me break. The anointing penetrated through the thick darkness I was in. The demonic chains were broken; I now could fight to be free. I was bound to the point I couldn't even fight. You see, the force behind the entertainment industry is a crave to shine. It's a lust for the worship of man. It makes people a slave to a possibility of what they can be. The people who are trapped chase their lust for the power and the delegated control of the people that comes with it. The thing that motivated us was the deep longing of a desire of significance. The desire for accomplishments of self-exaltation made them do anything and to justify it as their destiny. That word from the prophet Raphael Green in the Kingdom of

The Force Behind the Stars

Light stopped the agendas that hell had planned for my life. The governments of the industry didn't rule my mind anymore after the power of God touched me. I finally was free from the force behind the stars, which was Satan.

He started in heaven as Lucifer, but wanted the worship that only was for God. He craved the position God held. He wanted his name exalted. He wanted to exalt his throne above the stars of God. He wanted to sit in God's place. He lusted to be the King of the universe, so God Almighty gave the word and Michael acted on it and kicked him out of Heaven. His name was changed to Satan and ever since there has been a war for the worship. He wants every soul to worship him and for them to bring him worship. After my visit with the power of God at Metro, I understood why he wanted me. I was a worshiper, a dancer, a promoter whose gift he perverted to advance his kingdom.

I could fight back now with the living Word of God which is the Bible. I could tell the force behind the stars that I QUIT! I got the strength that I needed to break loose from it all from Jesus. I made him my Lord again. By the power of the Holy Spirit, I could tell them to kick rocks. I told them they could live like zombies if they wanted to, but I tasted the living water that really quenched my thirst. It quenched my soul from the need to have to chase that life. I told them I was tired of knowing Jesus was the truth, but still accepting the lie of the world. I hated living like we were gods and didn't have to answer to Jesus when our short lives were over. I was done with keeping up the image,

playing the part -- in public, at shows, in clubs, and at

parties, but behind closed doors, I was crying and

wanting to kill myself and murder other people, too. I

quit. I deleted every phone number, business card, and

burned all my pictures. I packed up my house, gave

away a lot and moved. I left thinking, they could do

what they wanted to, but I would not promote

anything that feeds the force behind the stars, which is

music that made people lust for power, fame, love,

money, and to get the flesh to feel good at any cost and

for the god of their belly to be filled. I was free from the

pull, but I didn't know the damage that the force did in

me. I had deep pain, hurtful bleeding wounds from

operating in that Kingdom of darkness. I didn't have to

obey the command, but strongholds and the demonic

pulls of that force was still in me.

Chapter 9

DETOX

When you go through detox you go through a cleansing to flush out harmful toxins out of your body. That's exactly what I was trying to do in 2008. I was living in Tulsa, OK now. I moved there to get my life together. I told myself I would never go back to the things I did in the music industry. I would not be responsible for encouraging souls to get money while on their way to a real hell when they died. I was glad I left St. Louis because I was too weak for the atmosphere of St. Louis. Every city has different principalities ruling and Tulsa was definitely "lighter" than the gateway city. I humbled myself and let the Lord detoxify me from the music industry. I had to give up a lot for my freedom of doing whatever I wanted to do as well as the money.

I needed a church home in Tulsa, somewhere I could grow and be built up in faith. And I knew to get out of the industry and transition into living for the

Lord Jesus will require a faith walk. You have to learn that you are not your god, and you don't have to hustle or try to make stuff happen. You have to face the fear of running out and not having enough. A lot of the musicians got in the music industry because they hate poverty. They hate seeing their family not having money, or couldn't feed their kids. The pressure to provide for everyone, the obligation from the people who are depending on them to make it, to blow up and stay rich is a load that is put on them.

Most of them are carrying their family, their city, thousands of people depending on them to open a door. That's a heavy load, and most suffer in silence while carrying it. I visited a lot of churches and my big sister told me about one called Spirit and Truth. They were meeting in an event center at the time. I walked in and saw a prophet of God named, Brenda Todd on stage singing "Holy Ghost Fire." I will never forget that moment in time. The authority in which she walked in scared those demons in me. I heard the voices of murder, torment, perversion, rage, pimping, fear of going broke, and lust be quieted, when she sung. She was talking about the fire of God that could burn anything out of you that's not of Him. I had never heard anyone pray so fervently. It was hot and it hit everything on my heart at that time. I remember her binding up the demons and devils operating in the atmospheres. I remember the authority she walked in. I thought WOW! She must eat, sleep and drink the Bible. You can't walk in this type of authority and not know Jesus. I loved her the moment I saw her. I met her husband, Tommy Todd after the service, and he wanted to know about me. He welcomed me and didn't judge me. I loved them, and Sprit and Truth became my home. They were intercessors, true worshipers and taught the solid word. They were pillars of the body of Christ. I felt safe. I joined the next week, and I felt covered with the prayers from that church. Meeting them was an honor, and I could see they were true Shepherds from a hug or a handshake. I knew from Prophetess Brenda Todd intercession she always covered the people in prayer, so I knew that I would be covered, too. I was home; I needed this Jesus to be my God, not the music industry or the pressure of making money to live. Jesus take the wheel.... I surrendered!

I was attending Spirit and Truth weekly and working at a retirement center doing housekeeping. I had got in touch with a female rapper named Chyna Whyte on Myspace in the early 2008. It took her a year to call me. When we finally talked, we discussed working together in the music industry since we both had similar stories of leaving everything in the music industry for Jesus' peace. It started out as business, but we ended up becoming friends. We would pray together almost every day and encourage one another in times of trials and temptations. I thank the Lord for bringing her into my life at that time. No one can really understand people who came from that life unless you "tasted it." She knew exactly what I meant when I texted, pray...having withdrawals. I had a change life in

2009. I was not smoking, drinking, and was celibate. I was satisfied just working and attending church. I didn't realize your life could be changed, but deep in you there could still be demons who wanted you to do their will again. I was finally sleeping without nightmares every night. The flashbacks of the murders, scenes from the strip club, and drama I encountered from the industry had stopped.

It seemed everything was going well until I hurt my back lifting a lamp at work that caused me to lose my job. I was okay, then I lost my car, too. I started to get stressed out and didn't really know what I would do. I received unemployment for a while, but Spirit and Truth no longer existed because it merged with Greenwood Christian Center Church on the north land of Tulsa under Apostle Gary McIntosh. His teachings were solid, and his wife Debbie was the very definition of kind. I visited once, but didn't feel that I fit in there. It was people with cliques and little exclusive groups that I could not really connect with. I thought about how I used to be in the clubs in the V.I.P suites with high brand shoes and clothes looking at the people who were not a part of the group, and that same feeling of rejection from snobby people who claimed Jesus was not for me. I followed the Todd's, but I missed the realness and transparency of Mama Brenda and Michael Todd at the youth group "So Fly."

I stayed home and went to church when I felt like it. If I missed a Sunday, no one called or even noticed. I didn't need to deal with the same spirits in the music industry that was in the church. I got paid for doing it in the music industry, so what's the difference, I thought? I started to see different Christians sing secular songs, using beats of producers who I knew was "crazy" and living straight for the lust of money, but would add Jesus' name to it. It's like all the young people enjoyed doing the things I just came out of. I didn't understand or see the distinction between the two worlds. Then I met gospel rappers from all over who wanted me to promote them because they knew I knew everyone in the music industry. They wanted to be famous more than the famous people. I was confused and hurt because they used the name of Jesus. I told Stephanie who is known as Chyna Whyte what I encountered. She laughed and said that's what a lot of churches are about. It's religion, not relationship with Jesus. Some people in the church who knew Jesus was more crazier than people in the world. It was all a show, an entertainment performance with no love for the people. She didn't grow up in church, so she didn't know how to put up this loving Jesus act some people did, and then turn around and talk about you behind your back. She was too down to earth and transparent to play games. I didn't know how to deal with these religious games in church either. I had lost my job and car, so I didn't have a ride anyway. I remember Troy, Aeries, Tocayo, Raymond, and Natosha from Greenwood, now called Transformation Church always being willing to pick me up for anything. I appreciate them and their realness of helping me.

The Force Behind the Stars

I am grateful I linked up with an open mic called "Flow Zone," which was held on every other Friday. It was held in a building that was not finished and needed lots of work. I loved Kazi for his realness, though; he was the founder, so I "jumped" on board. Kazi was originally from Louisiana by the way of L.A. He was cool as the wind. I wanted to help, to be a part of giving a platform to people to showcase their gifts in the Kingdom of Light. I started promoting Flow Zone open mic in Tulsa, OK. The staff of Flow Zone were so creative and were funny people who I loved working with. Mary, Sharita, Vasey, Jonathan, Deidra, Troy, Melissa, Reggie, my good friends Jasmine and Cory started to help, too. We were all from different cities who brought different flavors to the table. I had an outlet were people who were my age would meet up and "kick it" on Friday nights. It was all clean fun and just straight fellowship. Students from Rhema Bible College, Oral Roberts University, and from different churches would gather as one to hear poetry, songs, raps and stories that were similar to theirs. I will always be grateful for Flow Zone. It allowed me to still do what I love, which is promotions.

My niece Esther had finished college and moved to Oklahoma in 2009 and we both understood the music industry. It was hard to find jobs at this time in Tulsa. Even people with degrees were working minimal wages. We prayed together; she understood a lot about what I had been through and where I was now. The Lord placed people around me who loved me and knew what I came out of. My friend Tiffany Love moved back to Tulsa from Atlanta around the same time also. She was back living for Jesus as well. We knew each other since high school and had partied together often. That was definitely my iron who kept me in line, told me when I was wrong, gave me food if I was hungry, and hugged me when I was sad. We were now serving the Lord together. Now that I look back, I had people in my life to help me heal, but I wanted everyone to be my friend. It just wasn't a reality. I was just focused on fun and people coming together. My emotional healing that I needed was not a concern of mine, but that was the source of all my problems.

In the fall of 2010 I was living off my unemployment. I was never content after the music industry. The lifestyle of being on the go, traveling, shopping, and just living life how I wanted was something I had got accustomed to. I still remember the conversation with my past. I was in my apartments called the "Villas at Yorktown" and went back in my thoughts of how fast money came in. I felt alone and stupid. I felt stupid for quitting and again the anxious feeling that I was missing something, hit me all at once. I went back to the comfort of a blunt (marijuana). I had linked up with a guy I met in my apartments who had been asking me to come with him and get high for some months. I went into relapse and started smoking and sexing again. I was idle and bored, so it was exciting to get out the house with street people. He was always willing to pick me up, and willing to buy me whatever I wanted.

He sold drugs and was from a gang called GD's. Pimps and hustlers was my company, but he made me feel special. I met a different guy at a party that same summer who was from California and he was from the gang called "bloods". He had just gotten out of prison, and I understood him and his story. He was fine to me, even though I never liked "chocolate" guys. His dad and mom went to Greenwood at the time and was respected ministers. I found my old habits coming alive again. I was physical out of the industry, but it was so deep in me. I had never fully broken all ties. I started to connect back with old sex partners, DJs, and my

Industry peeps. I just wanted to see them free, but how can I help them when I was still bound?

I remember smoking and thinking how I could get back to promoting again; I needed money. Could I really trust this Jesus I was serving? His people sure were messed up. The GD I was talking to was from Chicago had a kid and a couple of "chicks" here. His brother stayed in the same apartments as mine. I remember the first day in June 2011 being on the phone for a radio interview with a show called "Attitude Shift" and hearing gun shots out my window. I found out that night; it was his brother that was murdered. He took it hard and dealt with the pain by escaping with the coke and other drugs. I tried my best to be there for him, but he had a main chick already.

Seeing this murder made me wonder was it me who was always attracting drama to me. Everyone I seemed to know or was attracted to was drug dealers or felons. They all had serious anger problems, and carried guns every place they went. I ended up not talking to the dark-skinned guy anymore because he got a girl pregnant that I knew and used to hang with. From time to time, I would see him at a bar where we all hung out at called Torchy's. A friend I called "T" from when I was young hung out there, too. She would always beat up my brother, Jimmy for getting drunk and trying to drive. She was one who I knew had my back and always took care of me when I was drunk. She was brutally honest and I loved her. Her guy friend and mine whose brother had got killed were in the same gang at the time.

Tulsa really had changed since I moved to St Louis. In 2011, there were more murders and hatred almost everywhere. When the hurricane destroyed New Orleans a lot of people moved there. It was becoming a crime filled place. We started hanging together, me and T. We always had fun laughing at the drama in our life and just at our problems. I have always had more friends in the world who knew about Jesus, but loved sin than in the body of Christ. Even though we had our crazy times, I knew they had my back. If I ate, they ate. If I was "rolling;" they was "rolling." If they was paid; I was paid. It even goes back to my people in the industry. We all just wanted someone to be there for us, to have our back, and to be loyal. What people needed was a friend, not "sometimey" people. Living for Jesus wasn't the question, the question was are you loyal to me? Can you love me until I get free? Will you love me until I get this faith in Jesus thing right? No one I encountered was rooted in love enough to deal with me, or my people from the music industry. These churches were focused on the same thing the world was, making their name great. Man, I got out of the industry for nothing. There are pimps who are pastors, too.

Some use prophesies to pimp people for their money. The Word says leader should not be greedy for gain. I saw different pastors preach sermons to seduce silly women to leave their husbands and be with you. It was manipulation and charismatic witchcraft. I was not fooled easily, I know these demonic spirits all too well. They knew as well as I, they did not have any authority. The kingdom of darkness knows who is truly anointed and who is playing church. It was the first time in my life I really saw the church drama. I thought many nights about why I quit if I still had to deal with drama with the Jesus' people. I thought, I might as well get paid for it like I used to do.

It was just drama and hurt with people who claimed the name of Jesus, but really wanted to just get money. It all reminded me of my past life. I had opened that door up again because of stress. I started smoking and my mind would be thinking about the Jesus people. I would hear questions like, where were my so called Jesus' friends. I had no one to have my back, people didn't really call me when I lost my car. I would text, but wouldn't get any replies. The people who could run around the church and speak in tongues couldn't even love for real. I was just looking for a group of people to accept me, to love me if I wasn't driving a Benz, but their love was superficial. They were all about appearances and a show. I thought at least the dope boys checked on me, and was there with me if I needed them. It may have been about the sex, but at least they made an effort.

I heard the words of the rapper Lil Boosie, "Murder, Murder, Murder got keep my nine," speak over me, and I embraced these words. I listened to songs by people who were dealing with rejection just like me. I spoke those words out over myself and the atmosphere in my apartment. Not only were the nightmares back, but it was 7 times worse. It was a spirit of death around me and those I rode with had hateful hearts. I didn't feel safe in my apartments anymore after the murder, so my big brother James let me use a pink and white gun. He always was very protective of me, and had just got out of the prison. I had the gun, but the next month someone stole it from my apartments. It was more drama and I hated all this murder, murder, kill stuff. I thought how did I get caught up in seeing another murder? It was time to leave, I needed help, because I was so confused.

I asked Prophet Brenda could I move in with her until I found another place. I had got a truck by then, so at least I was mobile. I stayed at the Todd's house and a lot of my torment stopped. I started to travel with them, and promote their ministry, Gap Standers International. It was a prayer ministry that brought people together to intercede. Miracles, signs, and wonders followed their works. They were solid people who really were living the blessed life. I witnessed her living sold out for the Lord Jesus and trusting Him to provide their needs. I would see miracles of people just saying the Lord told them to give her money, clothes, jewelry, perfumes, etc. For example: Someone gave her a mink coat and a Mercedes Benz. All their needs were met and they were in full-time ministry.

The faith she and Pastor Tommy walked in made me believe again in the Lord Jesus. I could see how

Jesus loved and took care of His own. The fear of running out began to fall off of me one day at a time. I remember the enemy proposing that I work and promote his agenda again through demonic voices and people from the Kingdom of darkness. I remember the mocking spirit saying, living for Jesus gets you nowhere. I remember them saying, I would go broke and be homeless if I didn't come back on their side to push the agenda of death on this generation. I remember them reminding me of my old status and constant daily cash flow. I said, "NO" I believe the Lord will supply my needs. I will not bow down to your demands or depend on your contracts that come with my soul being compromised and got results like blood sacrifices. It was not worth the money that I got from promoting the very thing that was causing people to kill and envy each other. I wasn't about that life no more. My faith was being built and my mentor Brenda Todd was always pouring life, prayer and the Bible into me. I didn't have to live in bondage to be rich. My Daddy Jesus owned the world, and He loved me enough to die for me. I decided to live in that truth, which made me resist the lies of the music industry.

Chapter 10

REHAB

I n rehab I was on strict supervision by the Todd's. When I came under their wing, I learned about this thing called accountability. I never had to answer to anyone about my personal life before. I remember days wanting to go smoke a blunt of weed or get drunk and Pastor Brenda would be on me like white on rice. It's what the mothers of the church call "you were on my heart". Her prayer meter would be on an all time high when I was being under attack. An intercessor named Natasha started to travel with us after two years, then Aeris, the Browns, and others came along as well. Natasha and Aeris were my battle buddies who held me accountable as well. We were all very sensitive and prayer warriors. They helped me walk out a lot of things. Stephanie from New Orleans helped me in rehab as well. She was never into the fame of the music industry when she was in it. She would always ask me what was there to go back to because she knew the drama I had been through. Jasmine and her husband, Cory, understood me and even to this day, they are my lifelong friends. I remember them taking me to the mental hospital to get medicine, so I could sleep. I was surrounded by a solid team.

You have to understand; it was a spiritual battle I was fighting. The Kingdom of darkness knew I was a leader, a promoter, and they needed me on their team because of my influence. My voice in the past influenced people to come deeper into darkness, but it was originally given to me to call people out of the Kingdom of Darkness. The enemy had perverted it. The demonic Kingdom was not letting go easy. With every godly relationship that the Lord brought me into, more chains of darkness fell off. The people who helped me get and stay free had to be full of love and long suffering. It was four years of traveling with the Todd's until I was introduced to Kingdom Keys Ministries. I would always hear Pastor Brenda saying "Esther, you can't be flipping like a fish in and out of living for Jesus." I would go a year doing right, then all of a sudden, I got "picked" back up. I wanted to do right, but I was filled with demons. I yearned for the lust of the world. It was hell from my past life still in me. I will never forget hearing a message about demonic contracts in the kingdom of darkness.

A pastor named Natacha Byrams spoke one Sunday at Kingdom Keys on 64th and Peoria, but to the "hood," we called it "61". She explained to us how we could be picked up at any time if we had unfinished business in the Kingdom of darkness. She said it was like a natural warrant. She taught on demonic calendars, and why around the same time every year or weekend something just comes to pull on you. I cried so much in the next six months under her ministry. The Lord used Kingdom Keys to deliver me from lots of demons I let in through sin, and I was healed from deep, deep wounds. I decided to take her counseling classes, because she explained, I needed to face the trauma in my life. For me, it took a fight to stop obeying the pull of my old ways again. I remember thinking, I am going back to my old life because I don't want to fight anymore. I started going to a bar called, "The Big Easy." I thought I had made friends there. We would get drunk and talk out our problems. Every time I would disobey the Lord, the door of sin would have me like a sitting duck to Satan. He came in one time stole my truck, my phone, my money and my licenses. I got a DUI one night from a club and spent 14 hours in a jail in Tulsa called David L. Moss. I finally learned my lesson the hard way. I would hear Pastor Natcha tell us by the Holy Spirit to take off our running shoes and surrender. When I did He came to me to heal me from what I didn't understand. Pastor Brenda told me that it was good that I finally learned my lesson. I thought about who God placed in my life and I was grateful, but they were heavy hitters, who did not play games with Satan. These women of God took their walk serious, and that same mindset started to rub off on me. It is true; it's all about the company you keep. I gave up on my way, and I finally surrendered.

The Force Behind the Stars

In rehab, I was instructed to stop traveling for some time and allow God to heal me from my hurts. Pastor Brenda agreed and I was sat down, so I could get it right. Pastor Brenda said she loved me, and she won't use me just for my gift of promotion, she wants me healed for real. She advised me to get cross-training from Pastor Natacha. I was covered in this season of my life where I could finally heal. Kingdom keys' people were like family. They were a small church, but it was like the book of Acts in the Bible. I would see her disperse the offering to anyone in need. I saw her teach on love and walk in it. It takes real Agape love to deal with people from the streets. They can tell if you love them or not. Her love walk made me cry; it made me realize there is a remnant living out the Word of

God for real. The love of God she walked in makes you feel like you are important, like you matter. Her prayer meetings were like nothing I had ever seen. Her leaders loved each other and had her back. The unity and oneness was amazing. I was so relieved to be with people who had a Kingdom mentality. She understood you had to buy the land. They were debt-free and never begged for money. She never once said if we didn't give the church wouldn't be opened. I never felt manipulation from her about money. There was no pimping for the building fund. I was so happy to have met a Pastor who did not operate under the spirit of mammon. She knew about the influence of music, she explained about portals that open through demonic sounds. She taught me on celebrities and how it was a deity set up in them who craved the worship of man. I have learned so much about how to pray accurately and who I was fighting. Pastor Natacha taught me that it's a pure holy life that will attract things in the spirit to you. She said it's like automatic doors, you don't have to force them open; the blessings will come if you are walking on the right path. The blessings of the Lord makes you rich and adds no sorrow with it -- rich in spirit, rich in your mind, and as your soul prospers so does the things in the natural happen. Many are trying to get the blessing, to hustle with no character or just plain greedy for stuff, but I decided to forget about the stuff and focus on loving Jesus.

In 2015, I can truly say I am on the road to freedom. I still feel I am in rehab because I know I have more healing to go. I know I am free from demons who once ruled me. Demonic spirits of perversion, murder, destruction, adultery, and fear were cast out of me. I remember when I was struggling with more demons inside of me, which was revealed by the word of knowledge, and the Lord God almighty freed me. I had been bound for so long; I didn't care who was watching or where I was. I wanted to be free. I had to fight and not run. It was many times where the pull of the world, my old image of who I used to be in the world, and the glory of the world would entice me back. I would be transparent to those God had placed in my life, and Pastor Natacha and Pastor Brenda would double team the demonic forces for a TKO, a total Knockout. I could sleep with the lights off and not be afraid of the dark. I had face to face encounters with the demonic realm proposing to me to worship them, and work for them. They used to call my name and tell me they would give me anything I wanted if I would come back. People were calling my phone, "hitting" me up on social networks asking me to work for them at the same time. It was so much I never knew about demonic networking, but through the revelations from Pastor Natacha, I understood how they operated. I finally understood who I was for real. My name was Esther, and my identity was only found in God, and who He had made me to be. What I was to overthrow, what I represented in the spirit realm made them afraid. I finally connected all the dots. They didn't want me to be me, to be who God made me. It was on now, I was free from them on the inside and I could finally fight

back.

Chapter 11

WHAT NOW!

After I chose to leave that lifestyle, I had to get freedom and healing in my soul. I needed deliverance and my mind renewed. The demons I had needed to be cast out and I had to fill up with the word of God.

I was loosed from the pull from my past!! The spirits that would rise up inside of me were gone, also. I am so light now, so joyful, no more paranoia and fear. I am being anchored in my identity, and it feels good. I wasn't lonely anymore or depressed. It's like; I am a new person, a new creation. I was fighting back and taking ground for others as well. I had to understand the love Jesus really had for me. It wasn't based on what I did or didn't do. I was totally accepted and wanted for simply me. This revelation is still healing me today. I remember getting a revelation of who I was, and my purpose to tear down the enemy's works he had set up. Everyone has a specific assignment, area of influence, a place where they are called to. I am living on the straight and narrow now, but I must avoid the things that try to bind me up still. The word says lay aside every weight and sin, which so easily entangles us. I remember times of struggle were I would have to call Mama Brenda and have her stand up for me, when I was weak. I have a prayer covering and accountability now. I also have a part to do for working out my own salvation with fear and trembling, so I made fasting and prayer my lifeline. The Word of God plays 24 hours in my home. I would tell all my old connections exactly what it was, and that I would not play with fire. It's by the Lord's mercy that I can walk free, with not looking back now.

I want to encourage everyone reading this on how your eyes and ear "gate" have a lot to do with whether or not you will have a strong walk in God. The company you keep, the music you listen to, the entertainment you participate in has everything to do with your spirit being strong. It is like a computer, if you put garbage in, you will get garbage out. The music sets atmospheres for what will happen. When I would go into my withdrawals, I would put on a song that feed my mood. It feed my depression, sadness, or loneliness. I remember being in Prophet Brenda's house and wanting to get home to have a drink and play my sensual music. I needed to set the atmosphere that made it easier to sin. I remember the melodies calling me to listen to the comforting words that nursed my wounds. The music and my old celebrity friends would sing to the pain; they could relate to me. When I would feel alone, I always knew what artist to listen to that understood me. You can't listen to their music unless you agree with it. It was more than just their voice; it was the spirits behind it caressing me to come back into the web they wanted me stuck in.

You see, the Lord says He will sing songs of deliverance over us, and He does. His songs to refresh us, deliver us, heal us, and comfort us. They sing to, but the purpose is to put hell on your mind. To bind up your spirit as they feed you lies and solutions to your problems.

I had to realize that music was powerful, and one beat or song would trigger my emotions back into that place of lust, passion and desire. I couldn't hear all those other voices in the music, but then try to hear from the Lord, too. My heart was divided. I couldn't love what they sung about and love Jesus, too. How can light co-exist with darkness? How can I eat the table of the Lord and of demons? My body is a temple of the Lord and there can be no more mixture. So I made a choice to walk on the path of light. The path of life and to live out what I always heard preached. I am not doing it alone, I rely on the never ending supply of the Holy Spirit to enable me to live holy. I still have residue that the Lord Jesus is cleaning off of me, but there is a way out and I am living proof you don't have to die to get out. You can live free of the past!! "What do I do after I get out?" The answer is go to Jesus and get an understanding of His love for you. He will clean you up, surrounded you with people who will care for you, heal you, and supply your needs to live. Don't be afraid of going without food or shelter. The Lord knows what you need, and all He needs is a "YES, I surrender" from you. If you stop trying to be your own god, and bow to His Lordship, the rest is a done deal.

Chapter 12

WORDS OF HOPE

To everyone reading this, my purpose for writing this book was not to entertain you, but spread light on what the world magnifies and calls, "The Good Life." I wanted you to know the entertainment industry is not what the videos show you. It's people in that life on the verge of suicide, living in depression, and who are prisoners of their own image. I want to give a warning to the young people looking in just hoping and willing to do anything to "Blow Up," you may gain the whole world, but the cost is your soul. The price is not one you can afford to pay. YOLO (You Only Live Once) is a lie, you actually live twice! Here on earth and you spend eternity either with the Lord Jesus or Satan himself. Someone has to pay for your sins, and if you don't believe Jesus paid for then you have to pay. You can choose today to believe that Jesus already died for you, so you don't have to experience the second death, which is hell. The life of sin is hard. Aren't you tired of just existing, but not really living?? There is no peace for the wicked, choose life in Jesus, choose to worship Him. Choose life! Choose to use your gift for Him, and His will. We are in a war young people and your life, your soul is what the enemy is after. I wrote this for you.

To every rapper I ever met or promoted, to every stripper, every model, my fellow promoter, to all my DJ's, every prostitute, every trick who has given their self to these men, and every music industry person who knew me, I LOVE YOU, and I apologize for not telling you the truth about Jesus. The influence you hold is a very serious one. Its influential and you will be held accountable on what you say, and where you lead people.

The music you speak over the people has deep lasting effects. The power of life and death is truly in your tongue. Words are seeds that will manifest in your life and in the lives of the people who buy your music. You tell me; it's just entertainment, but you were influenced by other musicians whose songs played a major part in your life's decisions. I ask that you think about how your music is affecting the thoughts of our future leaders. God is the only one we should worship and live for. I pray for you to see that the lies we lived in are deceiving this next generation. You and I know there is no loyalty in that world. I know the paranoia, the fear of losing everything. I know the torment, the dreams and the depression; you are all too familiar with. I understand the deep places of hurt and betrayal inside you, from you just trying to help your people. I know how the lows make you feel like dying. I say to you with open arms.....there is a way out! The way is Jesus. You don't have to live like you do. You have an outlet in me to deal with the demands of the industry. I care and see the pressure of this world on your shoulders. I Esther am interceding for you, and I am here for you. You must know, I was bound just like you. I was confused just like you. I was damaged with trust issues just like you. I needed to smoke and drink to comfort my mind just like you. I am living proof you CAN BE MADE NEW. This new creation stuff in Jesus is real. You don't have to be addicted to porn, lust, perversion, sex, money, drugs, shiny things, manipulation, and crave worship. No matter what you heard about Jesus; He is the real deal. My prayer over you is that the God of the earth, the God of Abraham,

Isaac and Jacob will visit you. I pray that everyone I mentioned in this book would meet the Great "I AM" before they die. Jesus loves you and He has been longing to heal you.

I want to elaborate on the issue that the entertainment industry instils in us. It makes us performance driven. It forces us to feel like we have to measure up to what the standards of the industry say to be accepted in it. It forces us to not want to come out of the house without some name brand clothing on our Ferrari's washed. It puts extra pressure on the women to have the best weave, biggest booty, and always have to look perfect. Women forced to get plastic surgery and abortions to keep the shape of their body in tip top condition. Anytime you are in this atmosphere, it will condition you to be performance oriented to get love. That's why God sent Jesus to earth. He sent Him because He knew we could never measure up to be good enough. You may feel like everything you do will not measure up to be good enough. I say to you; you are worth the innocent blood Jesus shed for you on the cross. There is nothing you have to do to make Him love you anymore or any less. You could have killed 1,000 people or rapped 15 kids, but the love of Jesus is the same for you. You don't have to get Jesus to love you or behave better, so He would. He simply loves you.

If you ever get this understanding you will live in true freedom! Think about it now! If you get a Grammy or if your music EP doesn't sell at all; Jesus still sees you the same. He still will want to be with you and talk to you. He doesn't need you to do anything, but believe in His love for you, because you are His. I want you to know; it's His love that cured me from this life of searching for fame. You can be made pure again. I want every stripper or video vixen to know that they can be made a virgin and washed clean again by the blood of Jesus.

I put all my business out in the world ONLY with hope of seeing YOU be set free from this life of fantasy and deception!! I want you to know the truth and be delivered. I wrote every line, so you can know there truly is freedom in living for Jesus. I love you, and you know my line is always open for you. "Hit me up, yo."

The Force Behind the Stars

I truly am a star, one who is a light in the lies of darkness. The glory, the honor, all the adoration of the deliverance of my very life goes to the ONLY TRUE and living God, and His name is Jesus. He is the creator of heaven and earth. I am grateful for the protection and cleansing that's in the blood of Jesus who has washed me from the smell, look, taste and influence of the world system. The great news to you, people who don't know Jesus is that HE is willing to do it for you, too. There is no other name under heaven that men can be saved, but the name of Jesus. You must know there is a payment for sin that you will pay now, and when you die for the life you choose to live. If you don't accept that Jesus already died for your sins, then you will have to pay.

To every women being used as cash cow in the entertainment industry, I say RESPECT is something you don't get from giving a man full of lust what he needs. A man telling you, either give him whatever he wants or you are gone is the lowest place you can be put in. He is controlling you and manipulating you into making you do everything he says, and then he will pay for your bills, it's not love. I say to every women I every pimped or promoted; you have value, you have real worth. The amount of dead presidents you get when they make it rain in the strip club can't be compare to your life. How dare you prostitute your beauty for money in the strip clubs, in the videos, in the magazines, and on the cover of flyers. You are worth more than that. You are fearfully and wonderfully made. You need deep healing from rejection and the need for attention. Most of you guys have missing father pains. It's so degrading to see us as a black race to still have our queens reduced to shaking butts on TV. Most of the women rappers are not role models. Many of them are in need of deliverance as well. I don't call you a b#$$$, a female dog, I call you a beautiful queen. My prayer is that one day you will see yourself as such. I pray you get up "off your back" and not allow the men to pimp you and reduce you to nothing. You shouldn't use your sexuality to use men either and manipulate them with children or with the power of sex either.

To the men who get value from the car they drive, the price tag of their clothes, or what hot new thing you can pull, you need healing also. You don't know who you are so you get your worth from your image, from your popularity, anything that feels that need to be accepted. Most of who I wrote about came from the ghettos, the slumps where you had to prove yourself to everyone that you are somebody. I think you are somebody without the two gold chains, the lambo cars, and three houses; you are a KING with or without it. The ache to be loved for you, is what I see in you. I see a King who had been abused, forgotten, rejected, and betrayed too. I see a man who needs the love of a true father to love him, and affirm him. I see the darkness, the numbness from all the pain. I see how the music industry has distorted your very identity. You are not who you have become. You can be who you were truly born to be. It's time for your freedom, for you to be free to be you. It's time for your deliverance. There is a way out, and Jesus is the ONLY way.

To all my people in the Kingdom of light I need your prayers as I go back like Moses to Egypt to declare the freedom of the people to worship the ONLY TRUE AND LIVING GOD. Please pray for these souls in the music industry who rule over our youth. My heart is the inner cities, the ones the music is targeted for, but I need your prayers as we go out. I will never forget all who helped me on my journey and the ones who are in my future to go out with me to deliver this generation from idolatry of these celebrities.

We will worship the Lord our God, and Him ONLY shall we serve. Let the true worship arise and every other sound be shut down. Come, Lord Jesus, come! Jesus is Lord of all lords and King of all kings! Jesus is Lord! May the Holy Spirit, my best friend, the great comforter bring us into all truth. Amen and Amen

About the Author

Esther R. Jones is a deliverance speaker who desires people to know Jesus, be healed, and set free from the agendas of the Kingdom of darkness. As a Publicist she travels throughout the United States and overseas representing her clients' brands. She was born in Milwaukee, WI, spent her adult years in St. Louis, and currently lives in Tulsa, OK. She has learned loyalty, love and teamwork being the youngest of 15 brothers and sisters. Esther Jones favorite quote is "Love never fails." Look out for her

next book to be release "I'm not crazy".

www.ingramcontent.com/pod-product-compliance
Lightning Source LLC
Chambersburg PA
CBHW051820090426
42736CB00011B/1580